Tend To Your Garden Within

Tend To Your Garden Within

A personal spiritual journey to know self, inspect beliefs, contemplate life, and lead a more joyful life.

Shervin Hojat, Ph.D.

Tiber Pubs, LLC
Austin, Texas
www.tiberpubs.com

Copyright @ 2008 by Shervin Hojat All Rights reserved.

This book may not be reproduced in whole or in part without written permission from the publisher, except by a reviewer who may quote brief passages in a review; nor may any part of this book be reproduced, stored in a retrieval system, or transmitted in any form or by any means electronic, mechanical, photocopying, recording, or other, without written permission from the publisher.

ISBN-13: 978-0-9818969-8-4

Library of Congress Control Number: 2008908536

This book is dedicated to Tammy, my wife, my partner and my best friend.

Contents

Contents	9
Preface	11
Acknowledgements	15
Introduction	17
Life	21
Self	41
Who am I?	42
Beliefs	52
Interrelationships	75
God	76
Inner Child	85
Other Influencers	100
Emotions	109
Fear	110
Love	118
Grief	126
Self-Pity	139
Navigations Within	147
Shamanism	148
Dreams	158
Awakening	169
Relationships	170
Insights	183
Reflections	221
Being Present	232
Journeys	245
Self-Healing Techniques	273
Index	287

Preface

Tend To Your Garden Within, is a compilation of edited excerpts of Shervin Hojat's thoughts, feelings, and his insights, since 2006. These writings were created in response to such questions as: *Who am I? Why I am here? What drives my emotions? What are my core beliefs? Where did my beliefs come from? How can I be more spiritual? How can I have a more joyful life?*

The root of our confusion of our true identity, is forgetting who we really are. As children, we form our opinion of ourselves and the world around us based upon our experiences, our perception of reality, our upbringing, interactions with parents and family, religious beliefs, and the society we were raised in.

We carry our childhood beliefs into our relationships, work, and family. Life events and relationships may not work as we thought or expected. We may feel emptiness inside. We may crave something higher than ourselves to feel and experience, instead of just reading about in books. We may not know how to react to change. We may not know how to trust ourselves. Most importantly, we may not know how to live with joy.

This book covers the evolution of the thinking process and emotional challenges of Shervin during his spiritual journey after his father's death. The main message of the book is to find self, to inspect beliefs, to recognize emotions, and to be able to respond to life's situations.

This book is meant to awaken and inspire you. Perhaps give you that *'aha'* which you may be looking for in your life. This book may also provide some insights into your relationship with your spouse, family, parents, and friends.

Tend To Your Garden Within consists of six essential parts:

Part 1: Life. Ponders on the purpose of life, fate, and destiny.

Part 2: Self. Covers two important topics. It explores who we think we are and what our beliefs about ourselves and the Universe may be.

Part 3: Interrelationships. Describes aspects of our relationship with God, inner child, adolescent child, and important people in our life.

Part 4: Emotions. Covers fear, love, grief, and self-pity. These emotions drive most of our behavior in everyday life.

Part 5: Awakening. The author's *'aha'* moments which describe: relationships, insights, reflections, being in the present, and his meditation journeys.

Part 6: Self-Healing techniques. Covers techniques that were used in the author's journey of personal growth.

This book refers to the 'being higher than us' as *God*. You may prefer to refer to the 'being higher than ourselves' as Goddess, Creator, Mother of Creation, etc, to better relate with the materials in the text.

Acknowledgements

I am extremely grateful to all the people and spirits, past and present, who have helped and enabled me to share this book with you. I would like to extend special thanks to my dad, Dr. Jamaleddin Hojat, and my mom, Azam, who did their best to provide me a loving and nurturing environment.

I would like to thank my teachers: Dr Melvyn Smith, who was very instrumental in starting my spiritual journey; Karen Hutchins, who taught me how to be grounded, to be kind to myself and trust my instincts; Gerry Starnes, who introduced me to the shamanic journey; and Victoria Vlach, who taught me how to understand my dreams.

To my editor, Jannie Balliett, A1 Editorial Service, who provided a polished edit in which the meaning of my words were kept true, if not enhanced, with her subtle changes in grammar.

I would like to thank Lindsay Cantler, who provided me very valuable and honest feedback on the organization of the book.

I am very thankful to all my friends, especially Cindi Koch, Jeannette Sutherland, Maria Noack, and Kathy Tracey for their continued support and encouragement. I am also thankful to all the people in the trance dance circle, shamanic journey circle, and dream circle that helped me to move forward on my journey of self exploration.

To my children, Aneesa, and Sam, thank you for being in my life. I have learned and grown, while you have grown and matured. My spiritual journey would not have been complete without your participation in my life. To my sisters, Shideh and Shouri, thank your for all your support, for being there for me, and helping me *see* my childhood and family conditionings.

Finally, I am truly grateful to my soul mate and spouse, Tammy, for her unconditional love, continued support for my journey, feedback on my writings, and by being at my side.

Introduction

This book arose from many years of searching for my spirituality and my life's purpose. The catalyst for this book, was my father's fatal accident in 2006 Tehran, Iran.

My father, while walking in a street next to his apartment in Tehran, was hit by a car on the pedestrian walk-line. He suffered a severe concussion, two broken legs, and one broken arm.

My sister, Shideh, and I traveled to Tehran. My father did not recognize us. We arranged for his care at his apartment until he could travel to the United States. His medical condition did not improve. In Feb 2007, we were told his situation was deteriorating due to bed sores and we needed to travel back to Tehran.

My spiritual journey kicked into over drive when I met my doctor, my homeopath, and most importantly, my spiritual teacher, Dr. Melvyn Smith.

I made an appointment with Dr. Smith, 150 miles away, a day before my second trip to Iran. He told me how I might become angry at my dad and God for what I was going through. He also suggested that I express my love for my dad on a mental level before my trip.

My trip to Tehran was delayed for twenty-four hours due to weather. Four hours before my trip, while lying in bed, I had an image of my dad, along with spirits of his mom, his dad, and his sister, by his side in a hospital room. I hugged and kissed him, and told him good-bye.

My father *died* while I was traveling to Iran. I saw his body at the hospital morgue when I had to identify him, something that shook me to my core.

I was born in Tehran. My father was a surgeon and my mother, a midwife. They provided a comfortable life for me. My parents worked a lot, but I was blessed with many loving family members who provided me love and care when my parents had to take care of their patients.

At age seventeen, I came to the United States to continue my education.

For many years, I focused on my family and my career. When possible, I tried looking for *myself* and my spiritual connection.

My parents began having marital problems in 1987, which placed a big emotional and psychological burden on me to act as the family peace maker. My parents never recovered from their problems. They blamed each other and got stuck in the past by always trying to convince my sisters and myself, that the other parent was wrong, while not accepting any ownership.

Since 2006, I have gone through many transformations. I have documented my thoughts, emotions, and inspirations, through poems and short articles. I will share some techniques that have helped me during my journey.

I share my spiritual journey and gifts of personal growth with you, to thank the Divine for all the blessings that I have been given. I hope this book will emphasize to value yourself despite your buried false beliefs, rely on Universe/God/Goddess for help, enlarge your perspectives in life, and to be able to know *yourself*.

My intention is to emphasize that we all have a noble purpose in this life. At times, we may go through self-doubt, fear, uncertainty about ourselves, and our worth. By becoming responsible to our emotions, connecting with the Divine and our higher-self, we can heal our past and change our future.

Life

Life is a process.

Purpose
07/15/07

Student: "Why are we here?"

Teacher: "We were originally part of God from whom we were separated. The purpose is to go through a *process* of finding our way back to God. The idea is, by finding your way back to God, you will become more than your original self."

"It is important to understand that the process itself is very important. If somehow you were put back with God, without going through the process, you would not have gained much."

Student: "What are the factors that will keep one separated from God?"
Teacher: "Belief, persistent self-pity, and despair."

Student: "Please tell me about *belief*."
Teacher: "Your belief in God and your role, is crucial how you live your life, and how close you feel to Him in your daily life."

Student: "Please tell me about *persistent self-pity*."
Teacher: "Self-pity is a God-given feeling that needs to be acknowledged and expressed. On a positive side, it will give us compassion. But in its negative side, persistent self-pity is the most potent thing that a human being can do to block receiving help from God.

Being a savior (refusing to deal with self), a victim (blaming others) and a martyr (I have more problems than others ...) is form of self-pity. "

Student: "Please tell me about *despair*."
Teacher: "Being in despair, helplessness/hopelessness, is the lowest vibration of all emotions. The person in despair does not have hope and does not seek help from God."

Student: "Thanks. This is very profound."

Gardener
06/05/08

Imagine that you are a gardener.

Many years ago, you were given a fertile land to grow your favorite flowers and plentiful fruit trees.

With the passage of time, you, your family, society, dumped trash and rocks in your garden.

One day, you answer your urge to visit your garden and plant something.

You may not be sure what. There are many beautiful options to choose.

You visit the garden. Your garden is filled with weeds. Below the soil are big and small rocks.

You may have decided that removing all the garbage from the garden is too much work.

You may be afraid to see what is under the big rocks.

You many not know how to begin tending your garden.

You may decide to just remove the weeds from the surface of the soil.

After some hard work, your garden *looks* good. There are no weeds on the surface.

Your garden looks like your neighbor's garden. Free of weeds.

You have done something to make your garden look better. You feel better about yourself.

You may plant flower seeds or flowers, or choose to plant small fruit trees in your garden.

You have heard it is easy to have a beautiful garden with minimal effort.

After a while, you notice your garden is not flourishing. The trees are not growing. The weeds are taking over, *again*.

You may think that your garden had a flaw when it was given to you.

You may think that you are not a good gardener.

You may think that is the best you can do.

You may hire a professional gardener to advise you on plant care or weed removal. He may even spray the weeds with chemicals.

The garden looks weed-free now. Your neighbors are also happy with your garden. You feel better now.

After a while, the beautiful plants are choked out again by the weeds.

You are frustrated. You have worked so hard on your garden, and still not much result.

One day, you realize that the weed's root system needs to be removed.

You realize that big rocks in your garden are blocking growth of your plant's roots.

You also accept that, by just keeping the garden weed-free, it is not what you really want.

You realize that if your plants have a strong root system, then the weeds can not flourish easily, and you do not need to work so hard to remove them.

You realize that you have accepted the big and small rocks in your garden. You also realize you may no longer need them.

You realize that the rocks are blocking the nourishment from flowing to your plants and trees.

You realize you need some tools to effectively clean up your land and garden.

You realize that tending to your garden is a continuous process, but a joyful one.

You realize that the Divine has always been sending water to your garden, nourishing your plants.

You begin learning how to work effectively on your garden and land.

As you cleanse the soil of your garden, removing the weed's root system and rocks, you realize a special closeness to the soil.

You may feel connected to nature more often now. You now have a special joy inside you.

As time goes by, you know what flowers and trees are best for your garden. No one has to tell you any more, what is best for your garden. You *know* it.

You spend less time on removing the weeds now.

You spend more time enjoying your garden and nourishing more beautiful things.

You realize your garden may look different from your neighbors.

You realize that all the plants and soil are connected at the highest level.

You smile.

You say, *"What a beauty."*

Fate and Destiny
05/27/08

What is fate? What is destiny?

Fate is to be born and eventually die.

Fate is to be raised in a specific family with their own cultural and economics characteristics.

Fate is the current situation we are in *NOW*.

We have many destinies in this life; some are more desirable than others.

Our destinies are forks on a road of fate, driven by our choices.

Finding a better destiny requires knowing self.

Better destiny is not obtained by looking outside of self.

Creating a better destiny requires a change in our perspective.

There are many perspectives we can hold onto.

One perspective is to rely on our instincts and reflexes, to survive life.

One perspective is to rely on our mind and our ego, to go through life.

One perspective is to rely on our contact with our soul, to live our soul's purpose.

One perspective is to rely on our connection to the Divine, to observe the game of life.

Like the law of gravity, any perspective that we hold, will have its own set of natural expected outcomes.

Different levels of perspectives provide different levels of choices.

Someone with a perspective of survival has a very limited choice.

Someone with a perspective of soul may have many more choices.

I may be fated to experience abuse as a child. I may be an abuser myself, or I may choose to rise above the hurt and help abused children.

I may be fated to be a neglected child. I may be hateful of my parents and society, or I may choose to have compassion for self and others.

I may be fated as feeling *not loved*. I may dwell on my situation, or I may choose to question my assumptions and change my perspective.

I may be fated to be in a closed society. I may stay closed-minded, or I may choose to question society's assumptions and reject what is not true.

I may be fated with a physical disability. I may feel sorry for myself, or I may choose to become a sports champion to inspire the *disabled* and *able* people in the society.

I may be fated to have been born as a child in an uneducated family. I may follow my parent's path, or I may choose to excel in what I love, show family and friends that anything is possible.

I may be fated to be a person with a family history of cancer. I may wait for it to happen, or I may choose to educate myself regarding my challenge, change physical and emotional habits, and perhaps never face the family disease.

We are fated as a mortal person. We may fear or ignore our eventual death, or we may choose to understand our soul's purpose and live life to the fullest.

Change in our perspective requires firm intention.

Change in our perspective requires continued removal of *old baggage*.

Change in our perspective requires eliminating attachments to anger, self-pity, and unnecessary beliefs.

Change in our perspective requires being in the *now*.

Change in our perspective requires healing *self*.

Change in our perspective requires asking help from the *Divine*.

Change in our perspective requires *courage* and *focus*.

When we start changing our perspective, we can see our best destiny clearly.

When we transform ourselves, new wonderful destinies, not imagined by us previously, will appear to us.

Garden of Life
09/19/07

You own your garden of life.
You can raise gorgeous roses,
or let the weeds take over.

To nourish the roses,
you need mental and spiritual energies.

You have all the tools available
to have the most exquisite garden imaginable.

Your energy is dissipated
by holding back feelings and emotions.
Expressing emotions irresponsibly,
judgment, gossip, guilt, shame, greed.

Stress of worrying of the future,
regret of the past,
rigid thoughts-
unchecked beliefs.

Dissipation of your energy
is feeding the weeds of your garden,
causing them to flourish,
and starving the roses you deeply value.

One day through an event, you look at your garden of life.

Asking yourself, "What happened to my garden?"
Asking yourself, "Where are my beautiful roses that I dreamt about?"
Asking yourself, "Where did all the weeds come from?"

You may believe that you had no control.
You may blame others, your bad luck,
or even God.

It is never too late to restore your garden to its beautiful potential.

Free yourself of what drains your spiritual energy.
Walk in the garden of life and smell the roses,
and attach yourself to the infinite source of energy.

Tunnel of Life
10/12/07

You were light and surrounded by vast light since the beginning.

You decided to enter the dark tunnel of life,
using the light of your soul to guide you in the darkness,
to experience *apparent* separation from the vast light source,
to find your way back to the light again.

After a while,
in the dark tunnel,
you ran into obstacles,
experienced many feelings and emotions,
received many bumps and bruises,
you forgot where you came from.

Your soul's guiding light started to dim,
you could not see your way in the darkness,
fear and beliefs covered up your guiding light.

You started thinking that darkness is everywhere.
You started thinking that being in darkness is due to your flaws.
You started thinking that you are all alone in the darkness.
You started thinking that you have to crawl in the darkness to survive.

You ran into people in the tunnel,
most people, like you, were afraid of darkness,
all having stories of why they were in the darkness,
telling you what existed in the darkness,
even though they could not see in the dark.

You also ran into individuals in the tunnel,
with many bumps and bruises,
whistling and content.

You asked them, "Why you are so happy?"
Their reply was that there was so much light out there.
"We remember how bright the light was before we entered the tunnel."

Life is a Process
07/17/07

Have you ever fallen in love?
Have you ever worked hard to get something you wanted?
Have you ever grown a plant?
Have you ever raised a child?
Have you ever nursed a sick person?
Have you ever taken a fantastic trip?
Have you ever eaten a great meal with friends?

What memories do you have?
What did you experience?
What did you learn about yourself?

Did it help you grow?
Did you grow because of reaching the destination, or while getting there?

What would have happened if you had reached your goals in a blink?
What would you have felt at that moment? In a month? In a year?
Would you have grown because of it?
Would you have experienced anything?

Life is a process.
A process of reunion with God .
A process of remembering of who you are.
A process that makes you grow.

A process that will help you experience yourself.
A process that will make you more than what you started with.

Life Movie
06/11/07

Have you ever watched a movie in which you felt you were part of the act?

You felt the happiness, sadness, love, hate, sorrow, and joy.
Every actor left an impression on you.
Sometimes, you took things very personally.

You experienced time and space.
You experienced a new identity.
You experienced separation from God.
You experienced feelings of a child.
You experienced some roles of the male, female, parent, sister, brother, son, daughter, husband, or wife.
You experienced the roles of victim and aggressor.
You experienced making mistakes and growing from them.
You experienced *deaths* of loved ones.

Sometimes you asked, "Why this life? Why this way?"
Sometimes you felt alone, and helpless.
Sometimes you had tears of joy, laughed, felt love, and connected.
Sometimes you felt one with a leaf, a bird, an ant, or a tree.
Sometimes you felt so disconnected; even hated dealing with yourself.

Finally the movie ends.
The acting on your part ends.
Each ending is different for the viewer; but all end.

It was like a short dream to you.
You are amazed how the actor had to forget *his* roots in order to survive as a human.
You now remember.

You come back to real self; entire acting lasted a blink.
You enjoyed the new experience; after all, that is what you chose to experience.

You are back to your true self.
You are back with God.
You are ready for another act

Self

It is fundamental to understand who we are. Our beliefs about ourselves dictate how we think, feel, and relate to the world around us. Our understanding of God, and how we relate to him, has a great impact on how we treat ourselves and others. Our ego also has an important role in our life which needs to be understood.

Who am I?

Why do you not want to know yourself?

Who Am I?
04/25/07

I woke up in the morning and looked at the stranger in the mirror. He looked familiar. He looked like my father; he looked like my mother. He reminded me of my sister.

I asked him, "Who are you?"
He answered, "Shervin."

I asked, "Who are your trying to be?"
He said, "I am not sure. "

"I am trying to be what my parents wanted me to be."
"I am trying to be what my teachers expected me to be."
"I am trying to be what society defined me to be."

"I am trying to be what my wife and children want me to be."
"I am trying to be what my work expects me to be."
"I am trying to be what a successful person should be."
"I am trying to be happy and in peace."

I said, "You can be safe and take a poll among your friends and use their input for happiness."
He said, "They look as confused as I am. How can I follow them?"

I said, "Find the happiest person at work and follow their path. "

He said, "I do not see many happy people. Besides, what makes them happy may not make me happy."

I said, "Follow your parent's path. Get advice from them."
He said, "They have done their best. I still do not see them happy with themselves. How can someone that has not been somewhere, take me there?"

I said, "Do you know who you are, or what you are?"
He said, "I do not know 'me' well. I have been busy meeting expectations of others, all my life."

I said, "Why you do not want to know yourself?"
He said, "Perhaps I am afraid of the unknown. Perhaps it is out of my comfort zone. Perhaps it is too painful to accept the fact that I have so many wrong beliefs about me. Perhaps I am not used to being in control of my happiness. Perhaps I have the false belief that I do not deserve to be happy."

I said, "Do not worry. You have started something good. When the student is ready, the teacher will appear."
He said, "Thanks. I enjoyed the talk. Let us do it again."

Ego
07/28/07

Ego is like a six year old child.

Ego has a limited belief system.

Ego's responsibility is to report to you what it sees.

You have given ego much more responsibility that it can handle.

You have asked ego to make decisions for you.

Ego hates you for this burden that you have put on him.

Ego feeds on its belief system.

If its belief system is based on fear… most of your decisions will be based on fear.

If its belief system is based on judgment … you will judge yourself the harshest.

If its belief system is limited … you will see yourself and others limited.

If its belief system does not love … you will not love yourself and others.

You define yourself as your ego,
because your ego believes it exists as a body.
You have accepted the ego's belief.

You fear death,
because your ego fears its own death.
You have accepted the ego's belief.

You do not like true praise and complements,
because your ego believes it is worthless.
You have accepted the ego's belief.

You resist love,
because your ego believe it is not worthy of love.
You have accepted the ego's belief.

You get frustrated when encounter difficulties,
because your ego believes it is alone.
You have accepted the ego's belief.

You become easily angered,
because your ego has certain rules that must be followed.
You have accepted the ego's belief.

You resist change,
because your ego believes only in familiar situations.
You have accepted the ego's belief.

You feel disconnected from God,
because your ego believes that you are separate from God.
You have accepted the ego's belief.

You fear life,
because your ego cannot comprehend the big picture.
You have accepted the ego's belief.

Hear your ego.
Hear the child.
Try to understand it.

Ask your higher Self if ego's belief is valid?
Is ego's belief working for you?
If *No*, change the belief.

You always have the higher truth within you.

Identity Crisis
03/31/08

Most people do not know who they really are.

We usually define ourselves by roles we play.

You may be a parent, a beautiful model, a girlfriend, a boyfriend, a lover, a smart worker, a spouse, a sister, a brother, a provider, or a helper.

What will happen to *YOU* when your role as a parent ends?

What will happen to *YOU* when your role as a beautiful model ends?

What will happen to *YOU* when your role as a girlfriend ends?

What will happen to *YOU* when your role as a lover ends?

What will happen to *YOU* when your role as a worker ends?

What will happen to *YOU* when your role as a spouse ends?

What will happen to YOU when your role as a sister ends?
What will happen to *YOU* when your role as a helper ends?

You are more than the roles you play in this life.

If you define yourself with only your roles, you will feel *dead* as your role ends.

Do not get attached to the roles that you play.

Do not put *YOU* in a limiting box.

You are more than what you narrowly define yourself to be.

My Ego
11/22/07

My ego, you know me as a physical body only.

My ego, you have tried to protect *me*.

My ego, you have tried to interpret events in life for *me*.

My ego, I realize that you have a limited perspective on life.

My ego, I listen to you but, know that your wisdom and perspective is very limited.

My ego, I do not need to *do* things to *be* myself.

My ego, realize that I am connected with the Universe.

My ego, it is okay to experience my emotions and cleanly express them.

My ego, it is okay to feel fear and anxiety.

My ego, it is okay not to have everyone's approval.

My ego, it is okay not to have everyone around you as my friend.

My ego, it is okay to acknowledge my needs.

My ego, do not discourage me from the path I am taking.

My ego, do not sow doubt and fear in my heart.

My ego, do not appear to me as my spiritual guide.

My ego, do not worry for my safety, if I do not follow you.

My ego, I am more than what you can imagine.

My ego, my heart is my ultimate guide.

Beliefs

Examine your core beliefs.

God's Name
10/01/07

God's name brings to everyone, a different emotion.

To some, peace, love, and bliss.
To some, intellectually feasible, but not felt inside yet.
To some, anger, guilt, judgment, punishment, contradictions.
To some, promised rewards.
To some, just a figment of imagination.

He cannot be described by words. Words are limiting.
He cannot be described fully by us.
A veil of our beliefs, frozen emotions, hurt, and ego, all distort His image.

He is not an abstract subject to be studied in a church, a temple, or a mosque.

He is what we see, feel, experience, sense, and hear, every day.

God is not an entity outside of us. Somewhere up there.
God resides in *ALL* of us.

To know Self is to know God.

God
06/15/07

Teacher asked me, "Do you love God?"
I replied, "Aha. Before I answer, I need to better understand what *God* and what *you* means?"

Teacher said, "I thought everyone knew who God was!"
I replied, "Are you talking about angry, revengeful, perfect, and all powerful God, or the God that would love and help you if you do what he wants, or the God that has unconditional love for all creation?"

Teacher asked, "What God is closest to your belief?"
I replied, "My *experience* of God is different than how religious books describe Him. There is much emphasis on *word* of God versus *experience* of God. Words are the lowest form of communication and are based on the writer's interpretation. Experiencing God is the ultimate way of knowing God in my opinion."

Teacher asked, "How does your belief fit your purpose in life?"
I replied, "I am part of God. In this life, I am mostly feeling apart from Him because I have forgotten my origin. I have been put on this earth to *remember* my origin. God wants us to experience Him and the only way is to be temporarily outside of Him. *If you are sugar, you cannot taste sugar.*"

Teacher said, "Do you realize according to most religions, you are questioning *words* of God and you will end up in Hell? Aren't you fearful?"
I replied, "I have been fearful about this for many years."

Teacher asked, "What is the ultimate goal of religions?"
I replied, "The ultimate goal is to be with God. Wouldn't God help me to reach this goal?"

Lean On God
05/06/07

Teacher Asked: "Why you do not ask God for help?"
I replied: "I do not want to be needy all the time."

Teacher Asked: "Do you utilize your legs to get your work done?"
I replied: "Yes."

Teacher Asked: "Why?"
I replied: "Because it is part of me and it is available to me."

Teacher Asked: "Do you use your eyes to get your work done?"
I replied: "Yes."

Teacher Asked: "Why?"
I replied: "Because it is part of me and it is available to me."

Teacher asked: "Do you feel needy when you lean on your eyes and legs to gets things done?"
I Replied: "Of Course *NOT*. This is a silly question."

Teacher Asked: "Why then do you feel needy if you ask God for help? Isn't he part of you and you are part of him?"

I replied: "You are right teacher. I need to internalize my verbal belief."

Teacher replied: *"Be Strong Enough to Lean on God."*

What If
06/24/07

What if YOU truly believed that...
You are one with God?
You are part of God?
You are worthy of God's love?
You are unconditionally loved?
You believed that everyone is from God?

What would you be?
How would you treat yourself? Your family? Others?

What if *YOU* truly believed that ...
You are separated from God?
You are on your own by yourself?
You are not worthy of God's unconditional love?

What would you be?
How would you treat yourself? Your family? Others?

What if *YOU* truly believed that...
You do not deserve to be wealthy?
You do not deserve to be happy?
You do not deserve to be free of guilt and shame?

What would you be?
How would you treat yourself? Your family? Others?

What if *YOU* truly believed that…
You cannot be loved?
You cannot love anyone?
You cannot trust anyone?
You just have to survive life's misery?

What would you be?
How would you treat yourself? Your family? Others?

What do YOU believe in?

What if *YOU* examined your beliefs?
What if *YOU* try to understand why you believed in them?
What if *YOU* throw aside beliefs that are not truly *YOURS*?

What if YOU …

Imagine
05/19/07

You imagine that you are alone.
You imagine that a large sum of money will bring you peace of mind.
You imagine that you can do it all by yourself.
You imagine that you are not wealthy enough.
You imagine that a big house and nice car will bring you peace of mind and happiness.
You imagine that you are not worthy of love.
You imagine that outside events will make you happy.

What if all are illusions?

What if you were not alone?
What if you did not have to worry about the outcome of events?
What if you had the ultimate guarantee that everything is taken care of?
What if you did not have to do anything to be worthy of love?
What if you had someone to lean on all the time?

Just imagine that you are loved, and the Universe will always take care of you.

Just imagine that you deserve the love of God.

Just ponder on what you have imagined.

Just feel the peace of mind.

Just feel the happiness.

Just imagine… it will become reality.

Hell
10/18/07

What is Hell?
Where is Hell?

Some believe it is down there.
Some believe one may go there after this life.
Some do not believe in it at all.

Hell exists on this planet.
Hell is not only a physical torment.
Hell is emotional and spiritual torment, as well.

How does it feel to be in Hell?

You will experience Hell when you assume things about people and are preoccupied with it.

You will experience Hell when you think you are the center of the Universe and everyone needs to cater to your needs.

You will experience Hell when you gossip about others and destroy their reputation.

You will experience Hell when you bring down others in order to feel *better* about yourself.

You will experience Hell when you allow your ego to rule your life and take things and events personally.

You will experience Hell when you are full of anger and fear, such that you can not concentrate during the day or sleep at night.

You will experience Hell when you focus so much on the dark sides of things, that you become part of that negative energy.

You will experience Hell when you are not your true Self.

You will experience the ultimate Hell when you feel separated from the Divine.

Emotions
06/14/07

Do you feel upset?
Angry?
Sad?

Check your thoughts...
Check your core beliefs...

Ask yourself...
Why do you feel sad, angry, or upset?
What thoughts have brought these emotions to me?

You may find several answers to your question...
You have certain beliefs...

Are these beliefs *correct* for you?
How did you arrive at them?
Do they still *work* for you?

Remember.
When you were a toddler, you were made to believe that:
"You should not cross street by yourself."
Where did it come from? Why?
Did it serve its purpose?
Is it still a valid belief?
Does it still *work* for you?

Examine your thoughts.
Examine your core beliefs.
Examine what is true for you.
Examine what works for you.

Beliefs drive your thoughts.
Thoughts drive what you will experience.

Buried Beliefs
10/29/07

I asked, "You feel sad?"
He said, "Yes."

I asked, "Why? Things have been going well for you lately. You feel happier and lighter."
He said, "What if I am wrong?"

I asked, "Have you been in this situation before?"
He said, "Yes. I have not taken the straightest path to my destinations. But they all have served me right. I have grown as result of them, and I am the person that I am now."

I asked, "Do you want to take the shortest path to your destination?"
He said, "Well, I am not sure. It matters how one gets somewhere and how one grows as a result."

I said, "Do you know that an actual journey, and *unwanted* detours, are part of getting to your destination?"
He said, "Yes, I do. It seems that I have a buried belief within me that 'life is a destination, not a journey'. This hidden nagging belief, does not serve my purpose anymore."

I asked, "Do you want to listen to your heart for direction?"

He said, "Yes, I do. But old programming and beliefs nag me deeply, so much that, *I cannot trust my heart.* The belief causes me to unconsciously judge my heart as incapable of trust and look for guidance outside of myself. This is another buried belief that does not serve my purpose anymore."

I asked, "Is it *okay* to listen to other people's heart and guidance, and not your own?"
He said, "No. I need to be responsible for my feelings and decisions. I can listen to others if I choose so, but the ultimate decision is my responsibility."

I asked, "How does it feel when you follow someone else's way, despite your heart's desire?"
He said, "I feel a deep sadness. No amount of public approval for 'following the crowd' heals the pain within me."

I asked, "Whose heart do you want to listen to for guidance?"
He said, "My heart. I am responsible to find my way with the Universal guidance. My heart is a candle in the dark tunnel of life, which cannot be covered up with false beliefs."

He said, "Thanks for the dialogue. I have work to do. I need to go within and purge the beliefs that do not serve my spiritual growth."

Self-Worth
11/27/07

I asked, "You do not feel happy?"
He said, "No. I am not happy. I feel depressed."

I asked, "Why?"
He said, "I have not been praised lately. I do not feel as worthy."

I asked, "Is that how you validate yourself? Counting how many times you are praised?"
He said, "Yes. It sounds very naive and silly to acknowledge it."

I asked, "What is the source of your agony?"
He said, "Probably the belief that you have to do something worthy of another's praise."

I asked, "Have you been sitting idle this past week?"
He said, "No. I was not. But, I did nothing that generated praise from others."

I said, "This is a difficult situation. You value your self-worth on what others see worthwhile in you."
I asked, "What if they do not notice the work you are doing? What if they are busy with their own issues? Are you going to be miserable until they notice you?"
He said, "Very good point."

I asked, "Does it mean that your adolescent child craves praise? Have you given him enough praise in your meditations?"
He said, "Not enough."

I said, "When in meditation, remind your adolescent child of his accomplishments, and praise him. Tell him of your current successes in life, and of your current situation with praise and acknowledgement."

I asked. "Are you going to evaluate your belief on self-worth as well?"
He said, "Yes. My self-worth is not based on how much praise I receive from others. This belief is no longer serving its purpose for me."

Should
08/18/07

My kids *should* respect me.
My spouse *should* understand me.
My manager *should* appreciate me.

I *should* have a comfortable life at age 55.
Parents *should* understand their children's needs.
Government *should* take care of me.

Life *should* be fair.
If I work hard I *should* be rewarded.
My family *should* love me for my sacrifices.

Where did all the *shoulds* come from?
Why did you accept them as facts?
How would you react if the *should* never happens?

Will you get angry?
Will you feel like a victim?
Will you judge yourself and everyone else?

Perhaps you mean *prefer*, instead of should.
Should will bring you mostly sadness, unhappiness, and pain

Do not attach yourself to specific outcomes.
Do your best, trust in God, accept the results.
You *should* not judge the outcome.

Thoughts
04/29/07

Teacher said, "Here are keys to the Heavens. Use them to get what *you* want."

I replied, "How do I use them?"

He said, "Be grateful for what you have. Check with higher-self to make sure it is what he wants. Assume you already have what you have wished; experience the feeling. Be specific and focus on the end result. Visualize and energize the wish."

I said, "Wow, that simple!"

He said, "This should not be news to you. You have been creating results of your thoughts all your life. Perhaps, you did not realize your power."

I said, "Most of my life I have focused on what I do not want."

He said, "The Universe answers your wish when you give it energy. It does not understand something that you *DO NOT* want. You always need to focus on what you want."

I said, "Can I just *want* and visualize more money?"

He said, "No. When you say I + Want + Money. The Universe thinks you want the feeling of *wanting money*. Instead, you need *choose* to *experience* having more money, if that is what you truly desire. Remember; *what you want, you can not have; what you experience, you can have.*"

I said, "I understand what is going on. This is a wonderful tool. But I am nervous!"

He said, "Why is that?"

I said, "If I do not know *me*, how can I wish what is best for *me*?"

He said, "You are on the path to know yourself and *remembering* yourself. God is always with you. *Be strong enough to lean on God.*"

Assumptions
03/31/08

Most people accept certain assumptions and theories as facts in their life and at their work.

We use those assumptions to explain other events in our life or work.

We assume that if we work hard, we will be taken care of.

We assume that a verbal belief in a higher being, will transform our life.

We assume that our co-workers will do their best at work.

We eventually run into some difficulty that tests our assumptions at work, or in our life.

We then have to make a decision in dealing with the difficulty.

We can give up, and come up, with many reasons why the difficulty cannot be overcome.

We can also give up and hope that the difficulty goes away.

We can blame others for all our problems. We may change friends or jobs.

We can create new theories about life and work, without discarding our original assumptions and beliefs.

We also can question our core assumptions. We can validate what is still true. We may learn a lot about ourselves.

How have you reacted to a difficulty lately? What core assumptions have you questioned?

Interrelationships

Our relationship with God, our inner child, our adolescent child, parents, friends, and teachers, have a profound impact on us. These interrelationships shape our beliefs, our thoughts, our feelings, and how we interpret and react to events in our life.

God

Remind me that imagination and balance, are the bridges between physical and non-physical world.

My Companion
10/19/07

Oh God,
my constant companion,
open up all my senses,
to better notice your signs and messages.

Oh God,
my constant companion,
wash away my ignorance,
and help me remember what I have forgotten.

Oh God,
my constant companion,
help me tame my ego.

Oh God,
my constant companion,
help me understand events in my life,
in perspective of the Universal wisdom.

Oh God,
my constant companion,
help me do the things based on
peace and compassion, not based on fear and anger.

Oh God,
my constant companion,
provide me strength to be kind
to myself and my family members.

Oh God,
my constant companion,
remove fear, anger, and self-pity,
from my heart.

Oh God,
my constant companion,
help me understand myself,
gain wisdom and enlightenment.

Oh God,
my constant companion,
help me to help others,
as others have helped me.

Oh God,
my constant companion,
help me not to be so busy,
that I forget you and your infinite blessings.

Lost
12/28/07

My God,
I feel that I am lost.
I am not able to listen to my heart clearly.
I am distracted.

My God,
will I accept the outcomes that I think may happen in the future, or try harder to change them?

My God,
I feel overwhelmed with things that need to be done at home and work.

My God,
I am distracted by events outside me that are impacting my peace and joy.

My God,
I question things that I should have done.

My God,
I feel like a leaf in a roaring river.

My God,
I know I can handle every situation you put in front of me.

My God,
help me strengthen my heart, rely on you, and let go of things.

Remind Me
09/13/07

Oh God, help me remember,
what I have forgotten in this life.

Remind me of the oneness of the Universe.

Remind me of my spiritual identity.
Remind me why I am in this physical body.

Remind me that I have a total of twelve senses.
Five physical senses:
touch, hearing, sight, smell, and taste.

Remind me that imagination and balance, are bridges
between the physical and non-physical world.

Remind me that I need to strengthen these two senses,
before I can remember my other five.

Remind me of the forgotten senses of
light, substance, warmth, motion, and voice,
providing me awareness and communication with the
nonphysical world.

Remind me not to deny my emotions and feelings,
as they will be blocking my authentic will.

Remind me to investigate
my belief systems, decisions, and theories.
Help me to remove false beliefs, theories, and judgments.

Remind me that I have access to the other world.

Remind me not to shut down perception of anything that is not physical.

Remind me that we are all connected to each other.

Remind me that I am not alone as an individual.

Remind me that we are all connected to You.

Oh God,
help me to arrive at a state of blissful joy in this life.

Responsibility
4/28/07

Oh my dear God.
Help me to become responsible.

Provide me the *willingness* to respond.
Provide me the *ability* to respond.
Teach me not to respond based on childhood fears or past experiences.

Teach me to respond in the *now*.

Remind me that *recognizing* anger, hurt, and resentment, is the responsible way.

Remind me that *acknowledging* and fully experiencing those feelings without judgment, is the responsible way.

Remind me that ignoring those feelings or *putting them in a box,* is not a responsible way.

Remind me that expressing my feelings by hurting others in any way, is not a responsible way.

Remind me that *expressing* my full feelings in a meditative way, is the responsible way.

Remind me that old feelings of hurt and anger, may
not be washed out right away.
Provide me the courage to release those feelings for
good.

Oh my dear God, let me free.
Oh my dear God, let me be in the *NOW*.

Inner Child

I will promise that I will not abandon you.

Child
05/12/07

Parents to a child are like *gods*.

The child does not think deep.
The child is naive.
The child is trusting.
The child takes everything personal.
The child takes everything literally.

The child tries to *fix* problems of his parents.
The child will do anything to bring peace and happiness to home.

The child will ignore his feelings.
The child will only focus on outside events for his happiness.
The child will not feel anything inside.
He just tries to survive.
The child is angry, but can not express his anger.

The child blames himself for family problems.
The child accepts the toxic shame of *rage* of his parents, as his own.
The child accepts the toxic shame of *emotional abuse* of his parents as his own.
The child accepts the toxic shame of society, as his own.
The child hates himself for this.

The child wants to grow up emotionally.
The child wants to be loved unconditionally.
The child wants to be loved,
but he does not know how to receive it.

The child wants to love,
but he does not know how to love.

The parents have not resolved their own childhood hurts.
The parents want to love the child.
The parents do not know how.

The child looks at his parents for help.
The child's cry for help, triggers the parents' memory
of their own childhood *cries for help*.
The child's cry for help is answered by shame
and guilt by the parents.

The children within parents have not matured.
They can only respond like a hurt child.

The cycle continues.

The child grows physically, but not emotionally.
He becomes an adult.
The adult child is still a child.
He acts up when the memory of his
childhood is invoked, just like his parents.

The adult child will have children.

The cycle continues.

Oh my child, help is on the way… you were always loved,
but you forgot…
you were always safe…
you can heal the wounds now.

Oh God, thanks for providing me the knowledge to see the cycle.
Oh God, the cycle has served its purpose for me… I have remembered.
Oh God, help me start the healing process.

Visit Your Inner Child
09/06/07

Relax.
Get ready to meditate.
You are about to visit your inner child.
You are about to start loving,
accepting yourself, while
feeling safe about it.

Visualize the house you lived in,
when you were five years old.

Enter the house,
go to the room where your inner child may be,
where you spent most of your time as a child.

Wait for your inner child.
The inner child may be available right away.

You may also not be able to visit with your inner child
on your first visit.

If the inner child does not show up,
do not worry.
He knows you are there.
Leave a gift for your inner child, with a note
stating that you love him, and that you will come back
later.

When the inner child appears,
tell him that you are from his future.
Tell him that you love him.
Tell him that you want to be with him.
Tell him that you are there to help.
Hug your inner child, if he permits you.

Let the inner child know that he has succeeded
physically, emotionally, and mentally intact.
You are his future and he has done his job:
you survived!!!

Tell him that he is not responsible for:
your parent's marriage, or parent's divorce, or your
mom, or your dad, or family problems.

Ask you inner child, "What is your wish?"
Anything that he asks, is fine to grant.
No harm can be done since you are meditating.

It is okay if you are asked to rob a bank.
You can make an arrangement in advance with the
bank president, so no harm is done to any one.

Remember, time passage for your inner child is not the
same for you.
A day for him is probably a few minutes for you.

If abuse has happened,
bring the parties in front of inner child.
Tell the parties, that the abuse has to stop *NOW*.
When you are ready to leave,
say good-bye to your inner child.
Emphasize that you will not *abandon* him.
Promise to come back and visit again.

Visit your inner child as many times as needed, as you have promised.

Toxic Shame
09/09/07

Shame is an emotion.

When it is used positively, it creates remorse.

When it is misused, it is toxic shame, and
it creates the belief in the person,
that he is flawed and defective as a human being.

Adults dump shame on children by,
physical, mental, and emotional abuse,
excessively controlling,
expecting perfection,
expecting over-achievement,
and teaching excessive mistrust.

A person with toxic shame,
runs away from true-self,
to cover up *defective-self*.

Rage is the most natural way to cover up toxic shame.

Toxic shame causes
self-doubt, loneliness, a deep sense of inferiority,
and inadequacy.

Toxic shame cannot only be dealt with psychologically,
it has to be dealt with
spiritually,
ultimately healed with the help of a higher power.

Visit Your Inner Child (toxic shame)
09/09/07

Relax.
Get ready to meditate.
You are about to visit your inner child.
You are about to start healing your toxic shame.

Visualize the house you lived in when you were five years old.

Enter the house,
go to the room where your inner child may be, where you spent the most of your time as a child.

Wait for your inner child.
The inner child may be available right away.
You may also not be able to visit with him on your first visit.

When your inner child appears,
say that you are from his future,
say that you love him,
say that you want to be with him,
say that you are here to help,
hug your inner child if he permits you.

Bring to the room, the parents/adults that forced shame on the child.

Tell him that the adults have dumped toxic shame on him by being abusive, or excessively controlling, or expecting perfection, or expecting over-achievement, or teaching excessive mistrust.

Tell the child that nothing is wrong with him/her.
Tell him that he is not defective or worthless.

Intervene, and stop the dumping of toxic shame on the inner child by his parents and adults.

In your meditative state,
give back a *sack of shame* to parents and adults,
saying, *I have shame that belongs to you*,
and we (you and inner child) are giving it back.

Go with the child to the child's bedroom,
ask for the higher-self to appear,
the power that has created you.

Ask the higher-self to take the child away to heal him.

The child will be taken away by the higher-self.
Wait until the child is returned by the higher-self,
he will come back.

When you are ready to leave,
say good-bye to the inner child.
Emphasize that you will not abandon him.

You may repeat this exercise a couple of times if needed.

Visit Your Adolescent Child
09/23/07

Relax.
Get ready to meditate.
You are about to visit your adolescent child.

Visualize the house you lived in when you were an adolescent.

Enter the house,
go to the room where your adolescent child may be,
where you spent most of your time as an adolescent.

Wait for your adolescent child.
The adolescent child may be available right away or,
you may also not be able to visit with him on your first visit.

If the adolescent child does not show up,
do not worry.
He knows you are there.
Leave a gift for your adolescent child, with a note stating that you want to be his friend, and you will come back later.

When the adolescent child appears,
say that you are from his future,
you are here to help him and be his friend.

Remember, the adolescent child's mind is chaotic.
He may grieve loss of his childhood.
He may grieve loss of closeness to his mother.
He may not understand changes in his body.
He may feel alone.
He may crave for love and want to be accepted.
He may crave for constant praise to insure his worth.

Adolescent child may be emotionally wounded.
Adolescent child may initially reject your help.
Adolescent child may want you to fail in your effort to help him.
Adolescent child may do everything to humiliate you.
Adolescent child may ignore you at first.

Tell him that you are his friend.
Emphasize that you are there to help, because you are from his future.
Emphasize that all the healing comes from future.

Do not be a parent to the adolescent child.

Ask your adolescent child what his wish is.
Ask him about his worries and difficulties.
Ask him if there is some activity he wants to do with you?

Share your thoughts and feeling with the adolescent child.
Share with him, on your successes and failures in life.
Share with him how your view on life has changed over time.

Be an advisor to the adolescent child, when asked.
Help him to find a friend with similar experiences and challenges.
Help him to find friends to fall in love with.
Help him by talking to his parents, regarding his treatment at home.

When you are ready to leave,
say good-bye to the adolescent child.
Emphasize that you will be back, and you want him as a friend.

Visit your adolescent child as many times as needed.
Remember, your interaction with the adolescent child may take a long time.

Do not give up; keep trying to reach the adolescent child.

Other Influencers

Something that no amount of money can replace.

Father
10/12/07

My dear father.

I have a mixed feeling regarding
your life and death.

For many years before your death,
you were physically next to me,
but I did not feel your spirit.

Now that you are physically not here,
I sense your presence when I focus on you.

I now sense your spirit, more than I sensed it
when you were here.

Now that you are not here
physically,
there is so much commotion regarding
how much inheritance I should receive.

I have already received my inheritance from you,
you have given me the biggest gift.

Your departure from this plane,
has awakened in me,
a great thirst to find myself.

Something that no amount of money can replace.

I am grateful for all your gifts.
Thanks for being part of my life.

Teacher
10/03/07

My dear teacher.

I came to you for help
when I was angry, in pain, depressed, and hopeless.

You sensed my soul,
while I was too busy to notice it.

You sensed my disconnection from God,
and helped me to get connected.

You felt my pain,
and helped me to acknowledge it, and start healing.

You felt my anger,
and showed me to how acknowledge and cleanly
express it.

You felt my fear,
and helped me to know and conquer it,
by telling me to have courage… it will be okay.

You felt my dependency on outside events and people,
and helped me to be independent by relying on *Self*.

You saw me upset about all my *troubles*,
and shared your *troubles* with me to show how one
grows.

You found me *irritated* by people,
and nudged me to *look inside*.

My dear teacher,
I am so grateful to God, and for having you
both light up my path.

One Year Anniversary
02/24/08

My dear father, it has been a year since you left your body.

Recently, you are coming into my thoughts a lot.

I have an image of you when I was eight years old, someone that I adored a lot.

You were a protector, teacher, source of energy, and zest to my inner child.

I am still trying to make sense of the last years of your life.

My dear father, I admire in you, the hard work and persistence you showed in your life.

My dear father, I admire in you, the open heart and passion you had for life.

My dear father, I witnessed your pain and emotional hurt, due to your shattered dreams.

My dear father, I felt your hurt, but could not make it okay again for you.

My dear father, I felt sorry to see you more often asleep than awake: your way of dealing with your emotional pain.

My dear father, although you are not physically here, your spirit is with me.

My dear father, I feel your energy and youth again.

My dear father, I felt your kiss on my neck. Thanks.

My dear father, I am glad to see you free and full of energy, again.

Mother
11/12/08

My dear mother, you allowed me to grow in you.

My dear mother, you did your best to protect and nourish me.

My dear mother, you were the world to me as a child.

My dear mother, I may not need you now, but the child within me always needs you.

My dear mother, the child in me looks to you for comfort and security.

My dear mother, it is so difficult to see you aging.

My dear mother, it is very frustrating not to be able to make you happy.

My dear mother, the child within me is mourning.

My dear mother, the child within me is sad.

My dear mother, thanks for being there for me.

My dear mother, no matter what happens; you are the perfect mother for my child within.

Emotions

Emotions need to be confronted and acknowledged. If we do not acknowledge our emotions, we will ultimately become our emotions. Fear, love, grief, and self-pity, are contemplated and addressed.

Fear

You have so much control over me.

Fear
06/19/07

Fear, our companion.
Fear, parent's way to protect their children.
Fear, mind's way to protect the body.
Fear, motivator of many.
Fear, we live with it all the time.
Fear, so close to us… we deny having fears!

What wakes us up in the morning? Fear or love?
What keeps us at a dreaded job? Fear or love?
What keeps us being nice to our friends? Fear or love?
What keeps us respecting our co-workers? Fear or love?
What encourages us to keep our rigid thoughts? Fear or love?

What encourages us to go to church or mosque? Fear or love?
What makes us do good deeds? Fear or love?
What makes us angry? Fear or love?
What makes us deny feeling fearful? Fear or love?
What makes us deny love? Fear or love?

Fear is a dis-ease.
Let us free ourselves from dis-ease.
Open the heart.
Listen to it.
Hear the inner voice.

Fear is gone.
Love is there.

Fear
01/14/08

Fear, you have so much control over me.

Fear, you have convinced me not to ask for what is mine; in case someone may get upset at me.

Fear, you have convinced me not to express my dreams; in case I may not reach them.

Fear, you have convinced me not to find out about truth; in case I am proven wrong with my assumptions.

Fear, you have convinced me not to love fully; in case I get hurt.

Fear, you have convinced me not to live my life and instead, focus on dying.

Fear, I now choose to look into your eyes.

Fear, I will embrace you and will get stronger as a result.

Fear, I will face you, and your paralyzing influence will disappear as the result of it.

Fear, you are teacher of my soul and enemy of my ego.

Fear, I choose to know you.

Fear, I choose to learn from you.

Fear, I choose to grow through you.

Power of Fear
01/22/07

Do you want to be empowered?
Do you want to be truly alive?
Do you want to feel free of bondages?

The solution is not to have happy thoughts, all the time.
The solution is not to ignore your fears.
The solution is not to focus on busy work, religion, self-sacrifice, alcohol, or drugs.

The solution is to face the sources that have so much control over you.
The solution is to stare in the eyes of your fears.
The solution is to know the source of your fears.
The solution is to consciously experience your fears.

The solution is to slay the dragon of fear.
The solution is to get your power back from fear.

The power is yours to take back.

Fear
09/27/08

Fear is in the air.

We may sense the fear in our body, even though
it may not be our fear.

Fear is reinforced by:
our limited beliefs, our chattering mind,
TV, radio, businesses, and politicians.

Do not take in the fear as yours.
It may not belong to you!
Use your free will and insight, to see if it is your
creation.

Fear is a very effective tool to strip you of your
free will and self-respect.

Decisions based on fear, may
by-pass our inner navigation and create harm.

Fear is a creation of our limited mind,
beliefs, and expectations.

Fear is strengthened when
we run away from it.

Fear is shattered when
we embrace it for what it is.

What Are You Afraid Of?
9/27/08

Is the basis of your fear based on what you believe?
Is the basis of your fear based on some unconscious beliefs?

Who is afraid?

The limited-self or the higher-self?

The limited-self has a narrow view of life.
The limited-self is like a six year old child driving in a cross-country car race.

The limited-self is distracted, confused, and scared.
The limited-self can not see well, is frantically busy, and thinks he knows everything!

The higher-self is focused, calm, and aware.
The higher-self can see the entire terrain.
The higher-self is limitless and confident.
The higher-self is void of fear, beliefs, and expectations.

Who do you want to be in your driver's seat?

Love

Let us take our journey together.

Lover
07/13/07

My beloved.

One who understands my aspirations, desires, without speaking.
One who accepts me, with no conditions.
One whose presence is always full of joy, love, and understanding.

I gaze into your eyes.
I see a vast ocean.
I see joy.
I see an innocent child staring.
I see myself.

Walk with me on the beach.
Listen to waves, wind, and birds.
Feel the sand.
Feel the water.
Hear God speaking.

Let us be in the moment.
Let us not take each other for granted.
Let us heal the wounds.
Let us forgive.
Let us remember.

Let us take our journey together.

Love
09/18/07

True love is unconditional.
Expressing love is part of our nature; it makes us happy.
To experience true love, one needs to give love.

When was the last time you expressed your love to
Yourself?
Your parents?
Your spouse?
Your kids?
Your family?
Your friends?

What holds you back from doing so?

You may not know how to express it.
You may feel that certain *conditions* need to be met first.
You may feel that it is a sign of weakness to express love.
You may feel that you cannot love anyone.
You may feel, that such expressions only required at a time of severe illness or death.
You may not even love yourself.

When was the last time you received true love?
How did it feel?

Do you know how to receive love?

Do you think you are worthy of being loved without *doing* anything?

Love is blind.

Love is *ACCEPTING* the way things are.

What is Meant by Love?
12/02/07

To some, love is being needed.
To some, love is being needy.
To some, love is having hot sex.

To some, love is being respectful.
To some, love is praise and flattery.
To some, love is safety.

To some, love is something you give and receive.
To some, love is being in a relationship.
To some, love is a reflection of self-worth.

To some, love is agreeing with the other person.
To some, love is spending money on the other person.
To some, love is being in a stable relationship.

To some, love is putting someone on a pedestal and minimizing self.
To some, love is something to strive toward, but may not get there.
To some, love is a feeling when you were a teenager.

To some, love is a vehicle to become *whole*.
To some, love is obedience to the other person.
To some, love is living happily ever after.

To some, love is a vehicle for spiritual and personal growth.

What is Love?
12/03/07

How do you know if you love yourself or someone else?

You need to be *doing* seven things, in order to create seven feelings of *being* in the other person.

Do you give?
Do you pay true attention to that person?

Do you respond?
Do you respond when you see the other person sad, etc?

Do you respect?
Do you honor the feelings of the other person?

Do you know?
Do you attempt to know the other person?

Do you become vulnerable?
Do you allow intimacy by being vulnerable?

Do you commit?
Do you have courage to commit even though you may not be 100% certain?

Do you care?
Does that other person matter to you?

If you have answered yes to the above seven questions, then you are doing the seven parts of *doing* to create love.

The other person in return, will feel seven *being* attributes of being loved.

Does the person feel secure with you?

Does the person feel pleasure with you?

Does the person feel vulnerable enough to allow honesty?

Does the other person trust you?

Does the other person have less fear of loss of love from you?

Does the other person feel intimate and caring with you?

Does the other person feel that you know her and accept her?

If you carry love, it will never let you down.

Love will not *fix* everything, but it can *heal* things.

Falling in Love
12/02/07

What is falling in love?
Why does one fall in love?
Why does one fall out of love?

Falling in love is so romantic and joyful,
it happens in an instance
by a look, or a smile.

What changes at the moment we fall in love?
Could it be that we stopped *looking* for love, and are experiencing love?
Could it be just feeling *love* in that moment,
changes our mood so much?
Could it be feeling *whole* make us so joyful?

What causes us to fall out of love?
Could it be the realization that another person can not fill the emptiness inside us?
Could it be we have turned to our old programming and beliefs?
Could it be it is not what we thought *love* to be?

It is rather easy to fall in love.
It is much more challenging to *be* or *stay* in love.

Grief

My little child, the only constant thing is change.

Grieving Process
09/30/07

We grieve when we lose someone or something dear to us.

Loss of parents, spouse, children, family, friends, or pets.

We may also grieve the loss of friendship, our innocence, unfulfilled dreams,
youth, career, and our childhood.

We may also grieve from anticipation of the loss of someone, our dreams, our job, etc.

When we lose someone close to us,
we may grieve for many things.

We grieve for not physically seeing that person.
We grieve for being alone.
We grieve for our mortality.
We grieve for our lost opportunities with that person.
We grieve for our vision of how things were supposed to happen.

Grieving has many stages which we may go through, some, or all of them.

The first stage of grieving is denial,
psyche's way to protect us to dampen the shock of the loss.

The second stage of grieving is anger at the person,
God, or others.
He should have taken care of himself better.
He should have avoided those friends.
How could he put me in such a situation?
How could God do that to us?
Why me? Why now?

It is healthy to feel and cleanly acknowledge your anger.
Do not judge your anger and feelings.

By denying your anger, you will just hide the energy in your body,
hence blocking the grief process, as well as causing many ailments as a result of the stored anger.

The third stage of grieving is rejection of other's help.
I will handle it.
I do not need anyone. I am strong.

The forth stage of grieving is guilt.
If I was nicer to him or her...
If I would have been a better a son, or a daughter, or a friend, or a partner.
If I could have, or would have, or should have, done that.

The fifth stage of grieving is bargaining.
What if I had him by me, the accident would not have happened.
What if I had taken care of him personally, would he have survived?

The sixth stage of grieving is depression.
This is anger that is layered and repressed, because we believe that we will get in trouble if we express it.

The final stage of grieving is acceptance.
Acceptance does not mean that we are okay with what has happened.
Acceptance is acknowledging that what we grieve is no longer physically with us.
Acceptance is acknowledging what has been lost.

As we go through the stages of grieving,
it is important to recognize our grief.
Do not try to stay at one stage for a long time,
otherwise your feelings may become *YOU*.

Little Child
01/10/08

I hear you little child.

I hear you, upset about many things.

I hear you say, *"Life is not fair."*

I hear you say, *"Can't good times last forever?"*

I hear you say, *"I want things to go my way."*

I hear you say, *"I want to be in charge."*

I hear you say, *"I refuse to accept change."*

I hear you say, *"I am too burdened."*

I hear you my little, five year old child within me!

My little child, you are not responsible for *me*.

My little child, you are not in charge of my happiness.

My little child, you are always protected.

My little child, I love you, and I will never abandon you.

My little child, you can not make rules for my life, and judge my life.

My little child, the only constant thing is change.

My little child, let me embrace change, and we will be free and happy.

Accept It
08/12/07

Have you inspected your beliefs?
Have you inspected your upsetting thoughts?
Have you noticed what drives you to do certain things?

Do you accept getting older?
Do you get upset at the thought of getting older?
Do you wish somehow you will not get any older?
Does it bother you that you are getting older?

Do not grieve life.
Live it.
Accept it.

Do you accept your eventual death?
Do you get upset at the thought of death?
Do you wish that somehow you will not die?
Does it bother you that you will eventually die?

Do not grieve death.
It is not YOUR death.
It is death of your body.
It is death of your limited ego.

Live.
Accept what it is… it will free you.

Do not dwell on past or future.
Do not dwell on *should have,* or *could have.*

Focus on the *NOW.*
Make the best of the *NOW.*

Mother Image
06/28/08

Depending on your age, look back ten, twenty, thirty, or forty years.

What memories does the word mother bring to you?

For most people, the memory is:
strength, kindness, love, and nourishment.

Mother was the person that allowed you to grow in her womb.

Mother was the person who was there to wipe the tears off your face.

Mother was the person who nourished and loved you the most.

Mother was the person you thought you could not exist without.

Now that your mother has aged, what memories does the name mother bring to you?

Perhaps, love, gratitude, and appreciation.

For some, there are more relationship issues toward mother.

Mother is no longer strong. It is hard to accept this new image.

Mother may be living in the past. You want to help her, but she is too rigid in her ways. It is hurtful not to be able to help mother.

Mother may project her fears on you, or on her other children. This is all she knows, how to protect herself.

Mother may say very hurtful things to you. It is hard to accept this new image.

Mother may lash out at you for not being good enough, while she is actually judging herself.

Mother has realized some fallacies of her beliefs. Now, she is agitated with her shift in reality. She is lost. You sense it, but what can you do?

Mother may have an image how old age may be. Most likely, what she experiences is different than what she had imagined. She is questioning herself.

Mother may be resentful of the past events. Maybe, she should have done something different when she was 35. She is re-living it everyday, and you can sense it.

Mother may be very sensitive. She may feel lonely. She may be taking many medications with many side effects. She is not the person you experienced as a child. It is hard to accept the new image.

Mother blames many things on people around her. She may want you to join her, to be a victim like her. She may feel hurt, since you do not agree with her views.

Mother may have a mild dementia. She may repeat things several times in one hour. You may get very frustrated. It is very difficult to accept this new image.

You may feel sad, angry, and helpless.

You are actually grieving.

You are grieving the death of the mother, who you knew as a child.

You are grieving the appearance of the new image of mother.

You are mourning the loss of your mother to age and time.

But you know deep down, her soul is still a loving and nourishing one.

You are also grieving for yourself.

You are grieving for the mother you still need to nourish your inner child.

You are seeing a fate you may have in twenty or thirty years.

But mother is giving you loving messages, if you are ready to hear:

My child, observe my behavior and words.

My child, do not take my words and behavior personally.

My child, do not react to me with anger and frustration.

My child, remember you are looking at me with *your* life filters.

My child, have compassion for me.

My child, I still love you, but *my* life filters have distorted my reality.

My child, do not resist nature; go with the flow.

My child, do not live in the past like me.

My child, do not mourn your youth like me.

My child, love and forgive yourself, unlike me.

My child, my words are hurtful, because I am hurt myself.

My child, you do not have to re-live my life; learn the lessons from me.

My child, live and love in the *NOW*.

Self-Pity

Persistent self-pity separates one from Universal grace.

Self-Pity
01/07/08

We all need to have a pity party once in a while.

We need to feel self-pity in order to have compassion and understanding for ourselves.

Persistent self-pity is a major source of blocking help from the Universe.

Persistent self-pity, separates one from Universal grace.

Persistent self-pity, manifests itself in us as three types of archetypes: martyr, victim, or savior.

As a child, we act like a victim to survive. We expect others to struggle for us on our behalf.

As a teenager, we feel like a martyr to numb our feelings. We pretend that the Universe is going against our wishes and desires.

As an adult, for our spiritual growth, it is no longer useful to act like a martyr or a victim. We need to take ownership for our thoughts, beliefs, and feelings.

How do you know if you are acting like a martyr?

Do you feel sorry for yourself?
Do you feel sad all the time?

Do you tell others, *"You do not understand me."*
Do you tell others, "*My burden is too heavy.*"
Do you tell yourself, "*My problems are irresolvable.*"

Martyrs are usually raised in families that have at least one martyr parent. Martyrs hurt people by their words and actions, hiding under the cover of self righteousness.

Another form of self-pity, is becoming a savior. Being a savior is a great virtue. But it is a problem if your motives of saving others, sacrificing at work, sacrificing for family, is to run away from your own needs.

All saviors in the end, will become martyrs.

We can leverage on the martyr in ourselves. It can give us strength in dealing with ourselves and the people around us.

Monitor your external and internal talks; are you a martyr? Or a victim? Or a savior?

Victim/Martyr
04/30/08

I am a victim. You may be one, or know someone who is a victim.

I am a martyr. You may be one, or know someone who is a martyr.

I may be offended if you call me a martyr. I may not talk with you.

I think my situation in life is unique, and you do not understand it.

I feel miserable inside and outside, but in reality, I do not want to change my situation.

I love talking constantly about my misery, to show that I am special and unique.

I have some hurt feelings from the past that I am not willing, or do not know how to let go.

I may be critical of my parents. I may hate them for how I felt they have treated me in the past. Sadly, I may treat my kids the same way as my parents treated me.

I will talk to you about my problems, and how bad they are, but I do not like to talk about solutions.

I may be very sensitive; I have many expectations of others; you can not expect me to behave the same way as I expect others to behave. I am special and entitled.

I feel I am a protector for my family, but nobody seems to notice my sacrifices.

If you try to help me, I will find thousands of reasons why I cannot be helped.

If you insist on helping me, I will tell you back off; you are not in my shoes.

I have a special defense mechanism to protect my victimized self; it is self-righteousness.

I typically make great sacrifices in time, and energy, in my own way, for my children, and community. You can not dare to criticize me for doing that.

I typically do not share beautiful thoughts with you. I am so focused on my misery, and self-absorption, that I am totally blinded to anything positive around me.

I am comfortable in my misery! It is a constant! I am used to it. I cannot help it.

I feel separated from friends and family. They do not understand me. The Universe does not understand me either.

I can not stand to see other people happy, if I am not. I make sure to *dump* my troubles on them, when I can.

I know how to manipulate well. It has become a survival mechanism for me.

I will not take ownership of any of my past misdeeds. There is always someone, or something, that has caused this to me, and is not my fault.

You may know me better now.

I made you feel sad. Perhaps you can now relate to some part of yourself.

Do not judge me. There is always a part of you that acts like a victim or a martyr!

Realize that you have used the victim mode for survival at certain phases in life, mostly as a child. Perhaps, you are not utilizing the victim as much as before.

Realize how I operate, and how I may make everyone feel miserable in a short time. I am an energy vampire.

Realize how I take energy away from you without giving anything positive back.

Do not argue with me. If you do, it proves that you are also against me, and do not understand me!

Send me energy to help myself.

Help me when I am ready.

Navigations Within

Shamanism and dreams were two important tools that helped the author tap into his subconscious. These tools allowed an understanding of issues at a deeper level, and enabled the insights gained to be used in his daily life.

Shamanism

Hear the familiar and the ever lasting.

Shamanism
08/04/08

Shamanism is the oldest form of spirituality that can be practiced by everyone, irrespective of their religion.

A shaman is someone who travels from the ordinary world to the non-ordinary world to retrieve energy, power, and information.

A shaman believes that all of creation has consciousness, and taps into universal consciousness to receive guidance and information.

A shaman can use many methods to go into a trance state, to travel to the non-ordinary world. Drumming, dancing, and chanting are some of the most common methods used around the world.

The process of going from the ordinary to non-ordinary reality, is usually called a journey.

A shaman can utilize many forms of guardians (energy forms) or protection in their journey.

A guardian may appear as an animal, plant, person, or a religious figure.

A shamanic journey is like a dream in which one is awake, and can direct ones actions.

A shaman in a journey has no preconceived idea about what is going to be seen and experienced.

A shaman in a journey may hear words verbally, hear words telepathically, sense things, or see images.

A shamanic journey requires a specific intention, an open mind, and use of imagination. One needs to relax intellect and expectations to connect to the non-ordinary world.

A shamanic journey is a personal journey through which the oneness of the Universe and the connection with sprits can be experienced.

Drum Beats
05/09/08

Get out of your head.

Open your heart.

Open your ears. Listen carefully.

Hear the drum beats.

Hear the familiar sounds.

Hear the heart beat of the Universe.

Hear the heart beat you have heard when inside your mother's womb.

Hear the drum speaking to you.

Hear the drum's stories.

Hear the drum's skin telling you the story of the animal that wore the drum skin, and gave its life to be heard in a different way.

Hear the story of the old tree that is part of the drum beater.

Hear the story of the drum maker.

Hear the story of the drummer.

Hear the spirits talking with you and among each other.

Hear the stories of many as *ONE*.

Hear the calm vibration of sounds and beats.

Hear the familiar and the ever lasting.

Totem
05/22/08

I took a class to find out about *totem* animals. These animals have similar energies that you may have. Totems can be great teachers and guides for us.

After going in a group meditation, several animals showed up for me.

I asked the lion, "Are you my totem?"
 He said, "No."

I asked the rabbit, "Are you my totem?"
 He said, "Maybe."

I asked the horse, "Are you my totem?"
 He said, "Maybe."

I was getting frustrated. I was not getting a firm answer from the animals in my meditation.

I asked the scorpion, "Are you my totem?"
 He said, "Maybe."

I felt something different about the scorpion compared to the others. I decided to come back to him later.

I asked the eagle, "Are you my totem?"

I felt something stronger in my stomach. All of sudden, my right hand started twitching for about fifteen seconds.

I had my answer. Either eagle or something like an eagle, was my totem.

My class instructor told us to keep an open mind about our totem; to read about them and to look for signs in the next couple of days.

I needed to find out if my totem was the eagle or hawk, within the next couple of days.

I went to the book store to read more about my totem.

I tried to keep in mind that I needed to narrow my totem to a specific bird.

While drinking my tea, I looked at the wall in front of me. There, a poster about *falcon* hung. I did not pay more attention to it. I wanted to know about the *eagle*.

I saw an acquaintance of mine in the bookstore named, Shahin. I had not talked to him in five years. I decided to mind my reading, and did not talk to him. I then went to the mall to get something to eat, and Shahin was within 15 feet of the area where I was eating lunch. I decided to chat with him there.

While going back to my car, it dawned on me that Shahin in Persian means falcon.

I opened Sunday's newspaper at home. All I could see was a headline in the sport section. *Flying like an Eagle.*

The next morning, I walked outside the house to get the newspaper. There were lots of bird noises outside. I looked up. I saw a black bird followed by a *hawk*. All the noises, were due to the birds fighting the hawk. Everything became quiet after the hawk left.

The next day, I went to a jewelry store to make a necklace from a stone. As I looked up, I noticed the store next to it, *Eagle Rehab Center*.

Later in the afternoon, while going to a business meeting, I saw a *hawk* hovering over the road.

Later that night, I attended a meeting at a coffee shop. I looked at the bookshelf. I noticed an American Indian statue with an *eagle* behind his head. I have been to this coffee shop three times before, and have not previously noticed the statue. I then opened a new magazine, it was about dreaming, and I saw an article about having *eagles* in dreams.

The next day after playing racquetball, I went into the locker room. The person that I played racquetball with, was out of the shower and getting ready for work. I looked at his clothing. It had an American Airline logo. On the right side of his shirt, was an *eagle emblem*.

Now I have seen eagles four times. Perhaps I can settle with the eagle as my totem. But, I also need to acknowledge the hawk. Whenever I take trips of self-discovery, I usually see the hawk in the sky.

What do hawks and eagles have in common?

They both have sharp and strong beaks. The beak reminds me to be careful of what, and how, I express myself.

They both protect their families.

They both signify rising to a higher level of consciousness.

They both signify communication between sprits and humans.

They both signify creation of a new vision.

What stands out for eagles?

Eagles can strike their pray with a force twice the speed of a bullet.

Eagle's ears are hidden, but they can hear well.

Eagles are opportunistic; they let others do the hunting first.

What does it mean to take an eagle as a totem?

It means take on responsibility, and power of becoming so much more than you now appear to be.

Dreams

Only you know what rings true for you in your dream.

Dreams
01/11/08

We spend 20% of our sleeping time dreaming. Roughly, for six hours of sleep per night, this is 3 years if you reach age of 70.

Dreams are messages from personal, collective, and/or the Divine subconscious, sent to us.

We all dream, but may not remember them when we awaken.

Dreams allow us to access untapped sources of wisdom that we are not typically aware of in our daily life.

Dreams allow us to learn about ourselves.

Dreams make us aware of our vulnerable areas.

Dreams point to challenges and their potential solutions.

Dreams point to our strengths and weaknesses.

Dreams allow us to rehearse behaviors in our daily life.

Dreams are sometime so real, that they can invoke extreme joy or fear, when one awakens.

Dreams are signs from the spirit world asking you to pay attention.

Asking For a Dream
02/18/08

We all dream every night, but we may not remember them.

You can request to have a specific dream before going to bed. Perhaps you have a question that needs an answer.

Formulate the question, or issue, in your mind just before going to bed.

While drinking a glass of water, tell yourself that you want to have a specific dream, and you want to remember it when you wake up.

You can also write the intent for your dream, on a small piece of paper and put it under your pillow. This signifies your serious intent to have a dream.

Have a journal available by your bed, so when you awaken, you can write down what you dreamt.

Write down your dream *as is*, without judging and evaluating. Jot down your feelings as well.

Pay special attention to your surroundings during the day. Be open. You may see something related to your dream on a billboard, in a paper, or on a sign in a street.

Over the next couple of days, read what you have journalized. Add any insights and thoughts that you may have received since your dream.

Make sure to somehow honor the messages of your dream in your waking life.

For example, if the message of your dream was for you to relax, you may honor your dream by perhaps making plans to go to a park after work, to exercise more often, to install a relaxing picture at work, or just putting the word *relax* by your bathroom mirror.

Dream Interpretation
02/11/08

Dreams are messages and metaphors from your subconscious.

Only you know what rings true for you in your dream.

Each metaphor can have unique or multiple meanings to each individual.

A car in a dream may mean different things to each person.

It may signify a means of transportation.
It may signify a burden of down payment or repairs.
It may signify your body.
It may signify a source of pollution.
It may signify a status symbol.
It may signify freedom.

You need to understand the meaning of the metaphors of your dreams over time.

What emotions do you feel when you think about the dream metaphor?

You can share your dreams with others; they can give you feedback, as *if it was their dream*. For example, someone can tell you the meaning of a car in their dream if they had such a dream.

Dream discussions may give you additional insight, but *YOU* need to derive the ultimate meaning from your dream.

Re-entering Dreams
02/18/08

We sometimes wake up from a dream upset, scared, nervous, or uncertain, about the meaning of our dream.

Perhaps, you dreamt that you were lost in an unsafe neighborhood.

Perhaps, you dreamt that someone was shooting at you.

Perhaps, you made some decisions in your dream, and the outcome woke you up.

You have control over the outcome of your dreams!

Sometimes, our subconscious mind brings up a dream to see if we are serious about what we verbally express. You can let the subconscious know that you are serious by re-entering the dream, and doing what you verbally express in walking life.

Re-enter your dream by focusing on the strong memory of the dream and the feelings associated with it.

If you were lost, imagine that you catch a taxi, or your spirit guide taking you to safety.

If you were shot at, imagine that it is part of a movie that you are participating in, and no harm will be done to you. You can choose the ending of your dream.

If you made a bad decision, imagine making a different decision in your dream and observe the outcome of that decision in your dream.

You may also visualize the outcome you desire in your dream, and step backward in time to see what decision caused the desired outcome.

After modifying your dream, you may feel much better and stronger.

You may feel that you have more courage to tackle difficult situations in your day to day life.

After all, you are telling your subconscious what outcome you desire in your waking life.

Role Play
02/18/08

Sometimes, you have a dream that does not initially have a clear meaning.

Perhaps, there are other people in the dream that you may not know.

Perhaps, there are animals or objects in the dream.

People, animals, and objects, are in your dreams to help you understand your dreams.

To better understand your dream, you can *re-enter* your dream, and do a role play.

You can re-enter your dream by focusing on a strong memory of your dream, and the feelings associated with it.

When you are in your dream, you can view your dream from the point of view of other people, animals, or objects.

How do the other people in the dream see you?
How does the animal in your dream see you?
What impressions do they get from you?
What attracts them the most about you?
What do they notice about you?

Do they have something to tell you?
What do they know about your dream situation and its context?

Write down the insights you receive from the dream while doing the role play.

Keep an open mind.

Listen to your small voice inside, with no judgment.

Awakening

Many "aha" moments have resulted from the author's insight into several important issues that everyone may face. Relationships, wishes, and aspirations, which are crucial in our lives, are contemplated. Reactions to events and others, which have a corresponding reflection to our internal issues, are addressed. Several of the author's personal journeys, by going within self to seek answers are also contemplated.

Relationships

Examine yourself first.

Emotions
07/15/07

Do not store your emotions inside your body.
Do not deny your emotions.
Do not judge your emotions.
Do not get attached to your emotions.
Do not become your emotions.

Feeling the anger is okay.
Feeling the sadness is okay.
Feeling the grief is okay.
Feeling the self-pity is okay.
Feeling the fear is okay.
Feeling the sorrow is okay.

Ignoring or denying your emotions is *NOT* okay.

Recognize the feeling.
Feel the feeling without judging it.
Express the emotions cleanly.
Release the emotions.
Turn your attention away from the emotion.

I Am Sorry
06/14/07

Remember times when you felt hurt by someone you loved.
They said that they were sorry.
You did not believe them.

Why?

Perhaps, you had heard these words when you were a child.
Sorry, I hurt you.
Sorry, I was not around.

You have heard these words before.
These words reminded you of your previous pain.

Perhaps, a sincere hug,
something more meaningful than words, will heal the inner wounds much quicker.

Blame
08/18/07

Check yourself carefully when,
you are angry, judging, blaming, criticizing, and
insulting to someone else,
for everything they have done to you.

Were you a *victim*?
What was your role?
What did you choose to *do* or *not do*?

As you relinquish responsibility for self,
you are more prone to blame others
for failing to fill up the emptiness within or,
for failing to provide for your own happiness.

Decisions
08/18/07

Do not get angry when you are tentative on a decision, and you disagree with decisions your partner or friend makes.

A decision may be
going to a movie, going to a restaurant, choice of dinner for the evening, or the next vacation.

Perhaps, you thought the decision was not worth fighting for.
Perhaps, you did not want to be criticized on your decision.
Perhaps, he was more confident in decision making.

Do not blame him.
Do not be angry with him.
He does not have any problem with his decision.

You were tentative on your decision.
You *chose* not to make your wishes known.
You *chose* not to get out of your comfort zone.
Take responsibility for your *choice*.

Co-dependency
10/21/07

Do you know anyone who solely defines their self-worth by the *accomplishments* of their family members?

Do you know anyone who solely defines their self-worth by how much they are needed by their loved ones, or their community?

Do you know anyone who solely defines their self-worth, by how worried they get about their loved one's situation?

Do you know anyone who wants to control someone else's behavior because they love the person and know better than him?

Do you know anyone who wants to control another person's life, so that they can live their own unfulfilled life by living someone else's?

Do you know anyone who does not try to solve their own issues, but is obsessed with the real and the imaginary issues, that their loved ones may have?

Do you know anyone who wants to control another person's life in the name of God, respect, duty, self-pity, or guilt?

Do you know anyone who wants to control another person's life by keeping them dependent emotionally, mentally, or financially?

You probably know such a person.
If you know yourself, and are honest; you may relate to some of these traits.

You may relate these traits to your spouse, mother, father, sister, brother, son, or daughter.

It may be very frustrating to see someone you love trying to destroy themselves and their family.

You may feel anger, resentment, or hate, for such behaviors.
You may take it personally while being treated as such.
You may live with the situation for many years, to keep the peace in the family.
You may want to ignore the issue, and hope it will go away soon.
You may feel toxic shame, or partially blame yourself for someone else's behavior.

Remember to have empathy for yourself, and the other person.
Remember, they may have had a difficult childhood, and current behavior is driven by many childhood beliefs.

Remember, they will not change until they are ready to change themselves.
Remember, the only person that can change, is *YOU*.

Remember them in your meditations.
Express your emotions to them cleanly in your meditations.
Repeatedly tell them, *"I love you"*, in your meditations.
Ask them in meditation, *"What lessons do you want me to learn from this situation?"*

Ask God to give you patience and wisdom in dealing with them.

Ask God to help them in *their* journey.

Expectations
10/29/07

Do not assume that your partner can read your mind. Communicate your emotions, feelings, and wants, without blaming him or her.

You tell yourself, "I do not feel loved. I need more love."
Is he/she supposed to know what you need?

Do you expect him/her to:

Hug you more often?
Call you in the middle of day?
Buy you something new every month?
Share his/her thoughts with you?
Praise you in front your friends?
Give you more space to grow on your own?
Tell you repeatedly, *I love you*?
Take you out for dinner?
Help you with cooking and cleaning?

It is your responsibility to let your partner know what you may need.

Of course, it is better if your partner asks you for your specific needs.

It all depends how such a request comes across. He/she may feel very defensive.
Do not get upset and say:

"Oh, you are not sensitive enough to read my mind."
Or,
"After all these years, you do not know me."

Just remember, you probably do not know your own feelings.

How can you expect someone else to guess and understand your feelings and emotions?

Forgiveness
03/20/08

We are taught that forgiveness is a great virtue.

Forgiving small things is easy. But how can you forgive someone who has abused you or has harmed you?

You do not have to forgive a person for *WHAT* they have done to you.

You need to forgive a person for *WHY* they may have done something to you.

We need to forgive ourselves first, before we start forgiving others.

You may have fallen short in your relationships and emotionally abused your spouse, and are now regretting your past behavior.

You treat your friends and family differently now, than you did twenty years ago, and you know *WHAT* you did then was wrong.

You now understand WHY you had those behaviors. Perhaps, you were insecure, scared, or did not know any better.

You can forgive yourself based on *WHY* you may have taken those actions. But, *WHAT* you have done does not need to be forgiven by others.

The same way you forgive yourself can be applied to others.

Why should we even forgive?

If you feel the need to be free, you have to forgive.

When you have not forgiven someone, it is like having them put in a jail, and you are watching and guarding them.

As long as you are guarding them, you are in the same jail cell with them with no real freedom.

Forgiving frees you from guard duty, and sets you free for more important tasks.

Common Denominator
02/01/08

You may not be able to trust anyone.

You may be agitated about all the drivers on the road.

You may have realized all your friends are unreliable.

You may have left several jobs for the same reason.

You may have been in many relationships and you considered your mates worthless.

Who can you blame or give credit, for the above issues?
Not all the people that you have contact with can be all bad and unworthy.
Not all the people that you deal with can be untrustworthy.
Not all the jobs can be from hell.

Do not quickly jump to conclusions about others worth or trust.

What is the common denominator in all the above issues?

YOU!

Examine yourself first.

Insights

Perhaps, the best wish is to be more present in the NOW.

Happiness
06/24/07

Do you want to be happy?

Do you need something to be happy?
Do you need someone to be happy?

Have you seen people with many *things*,
but not happy?
Have you seen people with *nothing*,
but happy?

Why do you think you need something to be happy?

Ironic
05/19/07

Student: "I am confused. There are many things happening in my life, and I am not sure how to deal with them."

Teacher: "What do you want the outcome to be?"

Student: "I am not sure. I do not know what I want. I do not know myself."

Teacher: "What are you doing in order to know what you want? How much time per day do you spend to know yourself?"

Student: "I do not even spend two minutes per day. *I am too busy.*"

Intense Joy
09/30/07

Do you remember the times that you danced with intense joy, as a child?
Do you remember the times you walked in the rain, with intense joy and happiness?
Do you remember the times that you took so much pleasure in hearing a story?
Do you remember the times that you took so much pleasure in eating an ice cream cone?
Do you remember the simple things in life that made you so happy, that you abandoned yourself in joy?

When was the last time that you recently danced with intense joy?
When was the last time that you recently abandoned yourself, in joy?

When will you plan next, to have intense joy?
What conditions needs to be met?
At your kids' graduation?
At their Wedding?
At your 50th birthday?
At your retirement party?

Why was it so easy to be intensely joyful when you were younger?
What has changed?

Perhaps, in your youth you accepted intense joy without *conditions*.
Perhaps, in your youth you were not so harsh on yourself.
Perhaps, in your youth you were not so fixed on your beliefs.
Perhaps, in your youth you believed that intense joy was as normal as drinking water.

Go back, and remember how easy it is for a baby to be joyful and laughing.
Try to remember the image of a smiling child.
During the day, try to keep that image in your mind often.

Doing Things
03/09/08

We greatly value *doing* things.

We *do* things to make us feel good, even for a short time.

We *do* things for enjoyment.

We *do* things to prove that we exist.

We *do* things to prove our worth.

We *do* things based on fear or anger.

We *do* things because we have to.

We *do* things to be happy later.

We *do* things so we can rest later.

We *do* things so we can have a legacy.

We *do* things so we can exert control on some events.

We *do* things so we can avoid emptiness.

Emptiness is something most of us run away from.

It is with or at true emptiness that we begin to see our real Self.

Gratitude
10/12/07

If you like to experience something that you desire,
you first need to imagine how it will feel having what
you desire.

You need to show your gratitude to the Universe for
that experience.
It may feel like that you are pretending.

Your ego and intellect may make fun of what you are
doing.

If you want to have abundance,
generate the feeling of having abundance.
Thank the Universe everyday for providing you
abundance.

If you want to have a loving family,
generate the feeling of having a loving family.
Thank the Universe everyday for blessing you with
such a loving family.

If you want to be healthy,
generate the feeling of being healthy.
Thank the Universe everyday for blessing you with
health.

If you want to have great co-workers,
generate the feeling of having such co-workers.
Thank the Universe everyday for blessing you with
such great co-workers.

Be persistent. You will succeed.

It does really work!!

Your Wishes
11/22/07

We all have been worried regarding our parents, children, and work.

Most people keep the worry inside, some talk it over with friends, family, and an even a smaller number, ask the Universe for help.

We usually focus and talk about our worries:
"I am worried about the safety of her trip."
"I am worried about my career."
"I am worried about my children's grades."

Notice that all the concerns do not actually indicate any desired outcome.

Perhaps, we believe that the Universe does not help us, or that we are helpless.

It is really important to focus on a solution to your worry.

What is your desired outcome?
How is the Universe supposed to know your desire?

We need to focus on the ultimate outcome,
do our best that we know how, to help the situation,
send protective energy to the people you are concerned about,
and ask the Universe for help in completing the task.

"I wish a safe trip for her."
"I desire a fulfilling job with the following attributes ..."
"I see him understanding class materials well."

Ask, and you shall receive.

Spiritual Journey
12/13/07

Once you experience joy and bliss,
going back to the old feelings is very painful.

It is not very easy to keep focus on *YOUR* spiritual growth.

Spiritual growth requires discipline, determination, and encouragement.

Spiritual growth is not a linear path.

Spiritual growth is not easy.

Spiritual growth requires constant presence of heart and mind.

You will be encountering *obstacles* on your spiritual path.

You will be tested along the way.

You will be strengthening *the muscle of your faith* on your spiritual journey.

Along the journey, clarity in your heart and mind will be firmly established.

Letting Go
12/19/07

Why is it, people experiencing near death, can experience intense joy, ecstasy, and love?

Why is it, we normally do not experience joy and peace in our daily life?

Perhaps at the moment of near death, we let go of everything that define *us*.

Perhaps at that moment, we are no longer bonded to our ego, thoughts, and programming.

Perhaps at that moment, blinders have been momentarily lifted.

Perhaps at that moment, we are seeing our true self, and the Universe around ourselves.

Perhaps we just need to die, in order for ourselves to be born to *our Selves*.

Perhaps we just need to let go of anger, greed, resentment, and surrender to love to be free again.

Attachments
01/10/08

Children have attachments to outside things in order to survive and feel secure; some are attached to their plastic nipple, some are attached to their specific clothing, or a blanket.

Although a blanket or a toy will never save the child, when in danger, those objects provide him a *feeling* of security.

As children get older, they carry with them, the same craving for attachments, however it is no longer okay to show physical attachments in public.

As an adult, we replace our childhood blanket and toys with more mental attachments, which are much harder for people to see and to judge.

Our adult *security blanket* may be: money, nice clothing, sex, food, family, community, or our fears.

Like children, we *feel* that our adult attachments will provide us safety and security.

As an adult, we drag our adult attachments with us until one day, we realize that our attachments have never kept us safe and secure when we were threatened.

Like a little child disillusioned with his blanket for security, we will be disillusioned with our outside attachments for our security and comfort.

This realization may be the start of a great journey in finding a real source of security and peace.

New Year Wish
12/31/08

Thinking of your New Year wishes?
Many things come to mind.
Family matters, money, work, or personal things.

The list is overwhelming.
Can it be done?
Are you worried now?

What if you can not accomplish the tasks, next year?
Will you still be *happy* if some of them do not happen?
Will you still be considered *successful,* if some of them do not happen?

Are you attaching your happiness and worth to outside events that have not happened yet, or may have already happened?

What would happen if you lost your job next year?
Would you consider your worth and value less?

What would happen if you got a big raise?
Would you consider your worth and value more?

What would happen if you could not afford a new car?
Would you consider your worth and value less?

What would happen if you could buy a new car?
Would you consider your worth and value more?
Many of the wishes we have, are based on fear and false beliefs.

Many of the wishes we have, lose their value gradually when we reach them.

Many new wishes appear to us, in order to keep the excitement and promise of happiness going.

What are your New Year's wishes?

Perhaps, the best wish is to *be more present in the NOW*.

Pain and Suffering
03/31/08

We are told that feeling pain in this life is normal, but suffering is not normal.

We may not have any control over the pains in life, but we do have much more control over our sufferings.

What is pain and what is suffering?

When you pull your tooth out, you may have pain.
When you think about the procedure three days
before it happens,
that is suffering.

When you have an exam, you may go through the pain of studying. When you think about your exam, agonize
before and after you take it,
that is suffering.

When you lose your job, you feel the pain. When you
worry about losing your job
and worry about it ahead of time,
that is suffering.

When you lose your parents, you feel pain. When you think about what you could have done, or what they
should have done differently,
that is suffering.

When you need money to feed your children, you feel the pain of poverty. When you think that Universe is mean to you, or feel you are being punished,
that is suffering.

When you are physically or emotionally abused, you feel the pain. When you stay the victim and dwell on it for a long time,
that is suffering.

When your mother says hurtful things, you feel the pain. When you keep dwelling on what she said,
that is suffering.

When you age and your body slows down, you sometimes feel the pain of aging. When you dwell on aging constantly,
that is suffering.

When you face your real fears, you may feel the pain of uncertainty. When you only try to deal with the symptoms of your fears,
that is suffering.

Valentine's Day
02/14/08

A day with many expectations.

A day that you are expected to show love.

A day with the expectation of receiving love.

A day when *love* is measured on how well you can afford things.

It is great to be appreciated and remembered on this day.

There are 364 other days that you may crave love and attention.

Who is supposed to love you and make you feel good inside all year long?

What kind of flower will bring you constant joy all year long?

What kind of chocolate will bring you constant joy all year long?

Who knows your needs the best?
Who cares about you the most?
Who can bring you joy all year long?

Do not search for the prince or princess out there.
Look in the mirror. It is *YOU*!

Have you cared about yourself today?
Have you gone within, to know yourself better today?
Have you told your inner child, *I love you,* today?

Happy Valentine's Day.

Self Discipline
04/09/08

We all desire to have self discipline.

We may express our wish to be more disciplined.

What is causing us to be less disciplined?

Most of us are disciplined enough to regularly go to work, take care of family matters, and watch our favorite TV shows.

What is it that we want to improve?

Perhaps, we wish that we could honor our wishes that nourish our soul.

Perhaps, we wish that we could read a book, take a class, exercise more, do gardening, or meditate.

What stops us from honoring our wishes?

We may say, "*I do not have time.*"

Some people may not have time because, they are working all day to feed their family. But, many people are not in this situation.

We have time to sacrifice for our work, family, and other causes. But we have little time to honor our wishes!

Perhaps, the first step to becoming more self disciplined, is to allocate a couple of minutes a day to ourselves.

Perhaps, we need to get a new belief that our wishes matter.

Perhaps, we need to realize that sacrificing for work, family, and community, is not a replacement for self-discovery, and self realization.

Perhaps, we need to acknowledge that our well being matters, as much as the well being of others around us.

Communities Within Communities
04/21/08

We are a part of many communities.

We usually associate ourselves with the *good* parts of our communities. We usually avoid associating with the *not good* parts of our communities.

We may express *shame* or *anger* toward the parts of the community that are *not good* or are *different*. We may blame some parts of the community for their failure to meet our expectations.

We may be proud of technological advances, sport successes, or our generosity. We may be ashamed of, or simply ignore, spiritual poverty, drug abuse, alcohol abuse, or other social problems.

Most of us are a part of different communities of religion, country, state, city, neighborhood, work, and family.

We are also part of the community of *self*. For example, we have an inner and adolescent child within ourselves. They sometimes control our emotions and actions.

We also have a warrior, destroyer, creator, sage, victim, innocent, and savior within us. They sometimes control our emotions and actions.

We also judge the community within us. We highlight the *good* parts within us, and we hide the *not good* parts within us.

We may also place parts of our community of self, in a shadow. Some parts, we may be afraid to face or acknowledge.

We may highlight our intellectual or monetary success, and hide, or avoid acknowledging our fear, hurt, and emptiness.

These communities all need to feel the oneness again.

The healing starts at the community of *self*, first.

We need to recognize all the parts within ourselves.

We need to acknowledge and accept all the parts within us, without judgment.

It is then the true healing of the communities can start.

We are then, ready to grow and help effectively the other communities outside.

Prison Guard
03/09/08

We are all prison guards without knowing it.

Like a prison guard, we guard against people who have done us emotional, mental, or physical harm.

As a guard, we visit the prisoners many times during the day, and remind ourselves of what they have done to us.

We may be angry at our spouse for doing, or not doing, things to us. We still hold them responsible after many years. We guard them in the prison.

We may be angry at our boss or co-worker. We guard them in the prison.

We may be hurt or upset with our mother, father, son, or daughter. We guard them in the prison.

We may be upset at our short comings in life. We guard ourselves in the prison.

We guard the prisoners 24 hours a day, by making sure they do not get away.

We punish the prisoners 24 hours a day, by taking their freedom away.
As a prison guard, we also have no freedom. We suffer with the prisoners.

Don't we want to be free of shackles?

Don't we want to be free from the prison for our own sake?

Rehearsal
03/16/08

We do rehearsals for many events.

We do rehearsals at school by doing homework.

We do rehearsals for sport events by practicing.

We do rehearsals for musical instruments by practicing.

We do rehearsals for exams by studying the night before.

We do rehearsals for interviews.

We do rehearsals for presentations at our jobs.

Rehearsals make us comfortable with coming events in our lives.

How do we do a rehearsal for our death?
How do we do a rehearsal for the death of our ego?
How do we do a rehearsal for the transition to the other side?
How do we do a rehearsal for meeting our higher-self again?

Dialogue With Guide
05/23/08

My guide asked me to make a wish from the Universe.

I said, "I wish not to work."

My guide said, "If you get in an accident, you can stop working. Is that what you are really wishing?"

I said, "*NO!*"

I said, "I want lots of money so I do not have to work."

My guide said, "You get money due to a law suit from someone injuring you, or someone dear to you. Is that what you really want?"

I said, "*NO!*"

I said, "I really want to work on things that I love."

My guide asked, "Do you know what you really love?"

I said, "I am trying to figure that out."

My guide said, "Perhaps you need to ask the Universe to help you find your soul's purpose and desire."

I said, "Thanks for the insight. I am glad that the Universe does not grant my wishes immediately!"

Attic
06/26/08

What is in the attic of your subconscious?

What have you hidden deep in your attic?

What secrets have you hidden there?

What thoughts have you hidden there?

What forbidden beliefs have you hidden there?

What painful memories are hidden there?

Have you visited your attic lately?

Do you have enough courage to dig in the attic?

You may get surprised at what you may find.

You may find confusing treasures hidden there.

You may find painful memories that may be a treasure for you.

You may find messy but soulful gifts there.

Are you ready to inspect what you have hidden there?

Are you ready to claim the gifts?

Imagine It
02/18/08

In order to manifest our dreams, we need to imagine them first.

Imagination mixed with strong desire, makes physical manifestation of our dreams a reality.

We need to tend to our dreams often.

We also need to cleanse our thoughts, and inspect our limiting beliefs regularly.

We need to imagine that our wishes have come true.

We need to live our wishes in our imagination, feeding them emotions and feelings.

Do you have a dream or a wish about yourself?
Do you have a dream or a wish about your relationship?
Do you have a dream about your retirement?
Do you have a dream about your future job?

How often do you tend to your dreams and wishes by imagining them?
Every day? Every week? Every month? Every Year?

Tend to your soul's wishes.
Take responsibility for your thoughts.
Do not allow your dreams and wishes to be without a gardener and nurturer.

Trash Collector
08/20/08

Do you pick up other people's trash when you are walking in the street, walking in the mall, visiting a hospital, or visiting a school?

Most likely not!

You probably will not pick up other people's trash and carry it with you.

If you are responsible enough, you may ask, "Is this trash mine?"

If *yes*, you would make sure your trash is dumped in a trash can.

In other words, you take responsibility for your own trash and may get annoyed when other people do not own their own trash.

How do you deal with your feelings?

Feelings can be like trash.

Have you gone some place and all of a sudden felt stressed and down?

Have you ever talked with someone and afterward, you felt miserable?

Have you listened to the radio or TV and felt bad, or out of sorts?

Have you ever asked yourself what caused your bad feeling or miserableness?

Was it my feeling, or other people's feelings around me that I picked up?

Do I own this feeling? Is it *my trash* or someone else's?

You do not carry other people's trash home. Why do you carry home other people's feelings?

How do you get rid of other people's emotional trash?

First, check if it is your feeling. If not, recognize and express that is not your own feeling.

Perhaps you feel the energy somewhere in your body.

Tell yourself, "I do not own this feeling, and I want to return it."

Feel the unwanted energy drain out of your body through your feet into the earth. Let the earth deal with the energy that you are not responsible for.

Chatter
07/16/08

Do you hear the chatter?

TV and radio are off, but you can still hear it.

Nobody is talking in the room, but you still hear it.

What is this chatter?

It is there when you try to go to bed even with the best headphones
on your ears.

It is there when you get up in the morning.

It is there when you are taking a shower.

It is there when you are on the phone.

It is most heard when you try to quiet your mind.

Chatter, you have been exposed.

Chatter, you no longer bring me joy and security.

Chatter, I now realize that you try to distort my reality.

Chatter, you are reinforcing the projection of other's fears onto me.

Chatter, I do not need your help or advice any longer.

Chatter, you want me to fear the future.

Chatter, you want me to feel sorry for myself.

Chatter, I now listen to my small voice inside.

Chatter, I do not need to have the answers to your continuous questions.

Chatter, I do not need to be this way or that way, to be okay.

Chatter, you have been exposed.

Chatter, be quiet. Let me BE.

Hurricane of Change
09/16/08

Change,
a nice concept.

Change,
we want to embrace it.

Change,
we desire it if it gives us security.

Life is a constant change.
Death is also a form of change.

Change is not predictable.
Change can be very painful, if we resist it.
Change can be upsetting, if we keep looking back at
what we had before the change.

Change can be very frightening, if we do not embrace
our fears.
Change can be very disturbing, if we judge it.
Change can be upsetting, if we let our mind assume the
worst.

Change tests our beliefs.
Change questions our assumptions.

Change forces us to face our insecurities.
Change forces us to visit our default mode of operation, when under stress.
Change gets us out of our comfort zone.

Change is like a hurricane.
If you resist it, it can destroy you.
if you take it personally, it will be Hell for you.
If you accept it, it can provide you new opportunities.
If you do not judge it, it will give you new insights.

Change, we want to embrace it.
Embrace change by being in the eye of the hurricane of your change.
Move with the change.
Observe the change.
Observe the turmoil around you all over,
as a result of the change.
Do not judge the impact of change.
Do not take the turmoil of change personally.

Be centered and at peace in the midst of the hurricane of change.
Become an observer, as you watch your movie called *"change."*

Have a perspective of an eagle, and look at the big picture.

Reflections

The outside world is a reflection of our inner world.

Agitated
02/19/08

I looked in the mirror.

I asked, "Why are you agitated?"

He replied, "The cats! They are so needy of love and attention. They will not leave me alone."

I asked, "Do you know that the cats are alone all day? It is natural for them to be happy to see you. Are the cats the real problem? "

"Please, think a bit before answering my question."

He replied, "I am tired of being needy."

I asked, "Is that why you do not like the cat's behavior? You see your own neediness in them, and do not like it?"

He replied, "Yes. I have disowned a part of me that is needy."

I asked, "The cats remind you of the part that you have lost?"
He replied, "You can say that"

I asked," Are you still upset at the cats?"

He replied, "No. They are pointing me to a part of me that I have disowned in order to be independent and strong. But, I know now, that I can not be a whole being by denying parts of myself."

Irritant Mirrors
09/27/07

Irritant mirrors are people who drive us crazy, irritate us endlessly, get into our head, and make us frustrated and angry.

Irritant mirrors are people who, if we can, we will argue with them endlessly to prove them wrong.

Irritant mirrors may be family members, friends, or strangers, who we want to change.

Irritant mirrors in reality, are our friends, if we hear the message.

Irritant mirrors show us parts of ourselves that we have judged and disowned.

Irritant mirrors show us our fragmented self, which we can reclaim if we choose so.

If funny people drive us crazy, most likely as a child, we judged being funny as something bad, and disowned that part of us.

If care-free people drive us crazy, most likely as a child, we judged being care-free as something bad, and we disowned that part of us.

If emotional people drive us crazy, most likely as a child,
we judged being emotional as something bad, and we disowned that part of us.

If curious people drive us crazy, most likely as a child, we judged being curious as something bad, and we disowned that part of us.

If self confident people drive us crazy, most likely as a child, we judged being confident as something bad, and we disowned that part of us.

Irritant mirrors help us to become whole again.

Only by being whole… can one have free will.

Our Story
12/05/07

We are all story tellers.

We all tell a story about ourselves, our perceptions, our life, our friends, and our family.

When we experience or witness an event,
we may all have a different story, because it is filtered through our perception and ego.

Our story is about *us*, our emotions, feelings, perceptions, and our needs.

Our story may not be the truth but,
it is the truth that we believe in, as we perceive things through the filter of our ego.

Our story changes if we are angry, sad, disappointed, happy, or peaceful.

Our story may be based on some limited experience, or most likely the story of others that we have accepted as our story.

Have you listened to your story lately?

Have you checked the validity of your story?

Have you checked your assumptions?

What story are you telling yourself?

Reflections
04/09/08

The outside world is a reflection of our inner world.

How we see the world events, can give us clues on how we feel inside.

If you feel that the Universe is not friendly and caring, then there is something in you that is not friendly and not caring.

If you can only see pain and suffering in this world, then there is something in you that is in pain.

If you feel that you are not connected with creation, then there is something in you that is disconnected.

If you know someone well and still do not trust him, then there is something in you that can not trust yourself.

If you regularly judge others based on appearance, education, or wealth, then there is something in yourself that judges you regularly on those traits.

If you are focused on *evil* in the world, then there is something in you that you think is evil.

If you do not notice the beauty in this world, then there is something in yourself that is being ignored.

Look in the mirror of the world and see your inner reflection.

Change Yourself
08/16/08

He asked, "What is up with you?"

I said, "I am really upset with my mom and sister. They keep questioning my actions on dealing with inheritance. They do not trust me."

He asked, "How does it make you feel?"
I said, "It makes me feel really upset. I feel like no matter what I do, it is *not good enough* for them."

He asked, "What can you do about this?"
I said, "I am trying to avoid working and talking with them."

He asked, "What does this situation tell you about yourself?"
I said, "I do not know!"

He asked, "Do you agree we create our own reality?"
I said, "Yes."

He said, "People come into our life to show us something, especially when the issue keeps repeating itself and you are upset about it."

He asked, "Are you doing the same things, to yourself that you are experiencing from your family members?"

I asked, "What do you mean?"

He asked, "Do you feel yourself *not good enough* no matter what you do in dealing with yourself?"
I said, "Yes, sometimes."

He asked, "Do you not trust yourself on things that you feel need to be done?"
I said, "Yes, sometimes."

He said, "Your family is showing you what you are doing to yourself. As soon as you change yourself you will not attract those energies to yourself any longer."

Being Present

Express your gratitude by words, emotions, and attitude.

Do Not Rush
08/14/07

When your attention is focused on the future,
or when your attention is focused on past events ,
you are not living in the *NOW*.

Do not rush
when you are with your loved ones.
Put your attention on them only.
Do not think of the past, or future.
Do not allow other things to distract you.

Do not rush
when you eat food.
Put your entire attention on tasting the food.
Do not think of the past, or future.
Do not allow other things to distract you.

Do not rush
when you hear the birds sing.
Put your entire attention on the bird's song.
Do not think of the past, or future.
Do not allow other things to distract you.

Do not rush
when you smell a flower.
Put your entire attention on the flower's smell.
Do not think of the past, or future.
Do not allow other things to distract you.

Do not rush
when you are praying.
Put your entire attention on the prayer.
Do not think of the past, or future.
Do not allow other things to distract you.

Do not rush,
when you hear God in the silence.
Put your entire attention on the silence.
Do not think of the past, or future.
Do not allow other things to distract you.

Do not rush
when you feel God in your heart.
Put your entire attention on the feeling.
Do not think of the past, or future.
Do not allow other things to distract you.

Do not rush.
Do not think of the past, or future.
Be in the *NOW*.

Rush
8/27/07

You rush to get out of bed.
You rush to say hello to your family.
You rush to take a shower.
You rush to read the paper.
You rush to eat your breakfast.

You rush to drive to work.
You rush to your meetings.
You rush to eat lunch.
You rush talking with co-workers.
You rush home during rush hour.

You rush to say hello to your neighbors in the street.
You rush to say hello to your family.
You rush to exercise.
You rush to eat dinner.
You rush to check E-mail at work.
You rush to go to bed.
You rush for the next rush.

What is the rush for?
What are you rushing to?
What are you rushing away from?
What is rushing you?
Who is rushing you?

Energy Drain
06/28/08

What are the major sources of your energy drain?

What do people spend most of their energy on?

Don't we spend most of all energy to either escape *what is*, or to change things to what *should be*?

Aren't we mostly occupied with comparing *what is*, with what *should be*?

Isn't most of our behavior driven by what things *should be*?

There is nothing wrong to have internal ideals to strive for.

Accepting *what is*, does not mean to do nothing to better humanity.

Accepting *what is*, means how we respond inside and outside ourselves.

Accepting *what is*, means not to be in constant comparison with what *should be*.

For example, your spouse, children, friends, and parents may not regularly call you.

This situation may make you feel angry, since it is different than what *should be*.

You have a preference to receive more phone calls from people dear to you. Nothing is wrong with this desire.

The issue is, how do you react to this situation internally and externally?

Do you feel anger toward them? Is your day ruined because of it? Are you in a bad mood?

What happens when they call you, after what you perceive as a long time?

Are you happy to hear their voice?

Is your anger unleashed on them directly, or indirectly, through your voice or interaction?

Are you still fixed on what things *should be* while talking on the phone with them?

Is your reaction now, making things better for future interactions?

What was most of the initial conversation about?

How much energy have you spent on this issue?

Can the energy be used in a much more productive way?

Wouldn't accepting *what is* be better?

Wouldn't talking on the phone without past memories, with full attention, be joyful?

How many other situations in a day, do you react in the same way?

When we constantly compare *what is,* to what *should be,* it creates contradiction, energy drain, and friction, which keep us away from being in the moment.

Did You Remember?
07/11/08

Gratitude is remembering and appreciating what we have now.

We usually do not pay attention to our current blessings.

We all have gotten up in the morning, and felt miserable.

We act as if we have lost everything we had in life.

What was your mood when you got up this morning?

Did you notice you are still alive while in bed?
Did you remember this blessing?

Did you get out of bed by yourself?
Did you remember this blessing?

Did you hug your loved ones this morning?
Did you remember this blessing?

Did you take care of your personal hygiene by yourself?
Did you remember this blessing?

Did you eat breakfast on your own?
Did you remember this blessing?
Could you see the sky, clouds, and birds?
Did you remember this blessing?

Did you listen to music?
Did you remember this blessing?

Did you walk out of your house without fearing for your life? Did you remember this blessing?

Did you feel the warmth of the sun on your body, this morning? Did you remember this blessing?

Turn your attention to the Universe and the gifts it has provided you with.

Express your gratitude with words, emotion, and attitude.

Gratitude helps us to stay in the *NOW*.

Today
06/08/08

Today can be your last day on the Earth.

Today can be one of many days ahead of you on this Earth.

Does it really matter how many days you have left on this Earth?

Imagine today is your last day on the Earth.

What is the smallest thing that you can do *TODAY* to honor your Self?

What is the smallest thing that you can do *TODAY* to show gratitude to the Universe?

What is the smallest thing that you can do *TODAY* to honor your body?

What is the smallest thing that you can do *TODAY* to listen to your emotions and feelings?

What is the smallest thing that you can do *TODAY* to show gratitude to your family?

What is the smallest thing that you can do *TODAY* to show gratitude to your parents?

What is the smallest thing that you can do *TODAY* to show gratitude to your friends?

What is the smallest thing that you can do *TODAY* to honor your dreams?

Small things like being gracious, lovable, accepting, and vulnerable, matter a lot.

Take time for small, important things.

Remember, all the big things are composed of small things.

Living and Dead
06/29/08

Most people dread dying since death is unknown.

Most people dread *living* since true living is total insecurity,
and is also unknown.

Anything that is unknown scares us. We always try to look for security,
and something that we have experienced before.

We love living in the past since it is known to us.

If we always live in the past, how can we be alive and living in now?

Truly alive people, live in the present.

Are you truly alive?

How does it feel to be dying physically?

The closest form of physical death, is psychological death to cherished and bitter memories of the past.

Have you psychologically died lately?

How did it feel?

It is like emptying a heavy load of trash from your back. It is liberating.

True living requires continual psychological dying, to cherished and bitter memories of past.

True living requires continued dying to worries of future possibilities.

True living only exists in the *NOW*.

Look around.

Go inside. Listen to yourself.

Listen to others around you.

Listen to TV and radio.

Who is truly alive?

If we are not alive now; perhaps death is a tool to make us truly alive again.

Journeys

Perhaps there can be less pain and suffering now and in the future.

Journey #1
01/12/08

I started by asking for protection from the Universe for my journey.

The intent of this journey was to meet my soul and get help for dealing with my fears.

Blindfolded, I listened to the music and started the journey.

All of sudden, I met someone very familiar, a dear friend.

Filled with joy and tears in my eyes, we danced to the music.

It was a dance of joy; the joy of meeting each other again.

The joy was very special; something that I have experienced several times in my lifetime, for very short periods of time.

We continued our dance, by dancing around a fire.

Next, I joined a group of three people dancing together shoulder to shoulder; with faces filled with joy, smiles, and eyes brightly lit.

After a while, I joined a bigger group of dancers going around in a large circle.

It seemed that we danced around a source of light.

After a while, I asked my soul to help me to deal with my fear.
He replied, *"NO FEAR."*

The next morning, I read a couple of pages of a book.

The discussion was about love and fear!

It stated that fear, is created by ego and karma. The universal message has always been, *FEAR NOT*.

WOW!

Journey #2
01/18/08

I started by asking for protection from the Universe for my journey.

The intent of this journey, was to understand why I am afraid of dying.

Blindfolded, I listened to the music and started the journey.

I saw images of being a small child; parents and family had a sad look on their faces while staring at me.

I felt their sorrow that I may not make it, and die (I became very sick as a child).

Later I saw another image while lying on my back; a group of people visiting me.

It looked like some kind of tribe. I also felt sadness in their faces.

Journey #3
02/13/08

I started by asking for protection from the Universe for my journey.

The intent of this journey was to get clarification and purification.

Lying on my back, I started the journey.

A hawk showed up as my power animal, on the other side.

He took me to a very tall waterfall. I washed myself with that water.

He then showed me how to soar in the sky. He taught me how to stay up, and look down below without fear.

As a drum was beating, I was free like a bird, and soaring in the beautiful sky.

Emotions overcame me. Tears started pouring.

I was so grateful that the bird was showing me how to be free.

My tears of joy, was not because I could soar the sky, but the fact that I am loved and blessed.

The bird shared part of himself with me. I sensed a great feeling of love and gratitude.

I was truly blessed.

Journey #4
04/24/06

I introduced myself to her.

I said, "I am Shervin, from your future."

She said, "Yes. You have been visiting me and sitting by me for the past couple of days."

I said, "I am here to be with you."

I said, "I am here to hear your story."

I said, "I will be with you when you transition to the other side."

I said, "I will be with you during the transition to reduce the pain of separation."

I said, "In exchange, I request that upon your departure you give me all the wisdom, memory, emotion, pain, and sorrow of this life time."

She asked, "Why?"

I said, "Some memory of your pain and emotion of your life time is with me. It is impacting my current life. I need to feel the complete emotion and pain. I need to acknowledge the pain. I need to understand it in its proper perspective."

I said, "I need to remember the wisdom of your life completely so that I will not re-live it again in this life time."

I asked, "Do you want to share your story with me?"

She said in a weak voice, "Yes."

She said that she had always wanted to be taken care of. She said that she always hoped someone would one day rescue her from life's struggles, protect her, and love her.

She said that one day she met a young and handsome warrior. She fell in love immediately.
She was in heaven when she was with him. She felt protected and blessed.

She said that one day her lover came to her and said that he needed to leave her for a war.

She said that she cried and begged him not to go. He had a choice to stay with her and chose to go to war.

She said that he told her that it was his destiny and he needed to go. He put his armor on, got on his horse, and rode off into the horizon.

I told her that I remember this image. I told her that I have seen this event in my dreams when I feel hurt and abandoned. I told her that this repeated image has made me search for her.

She was now very sad and emotional.

She said that she felt betrayed and not loved. She felt that she had done something wrong to deserve this. She felt that she was not worth being loved.

She said that she lost all the hope and energy for life after his departure. She said that she did not know what happened to him.

I sensed that her moment of departure was getting closer.

I hugged her. I felt her pain and sorrow in my body. I felt that she had a hard time breathing. I had a hard time breathing myself now.

I told her, "You have not done anything wrong. He loved you. He had to do what was needed for his personal growth. He died in the battle."

After a while, I felt her life energy leaving her body. A white light was leaving her body. I held her hands firmly, and comforted her in her transition.

After grieving for a while, calm and peace returned to me.

I was still sad. I needed to acknowledge the gifts I had received and transform the emotions into wisdom and insight.

I needed to acknowledge that some of the feelings of abandonment and betrayal toward my loved ones in this life, was due to her past life experiences.

I asked myself that what was the lesson for me?

I appreciated the beauty and love between the two individuals. I did not necessarily appreciate the intense pain and suffering.

She unrealistically *expected* that someone would take care of her like a child and love her.
She experienced love and being taken care of for a while. After that she felt abandoned and betrayed by his departure to war.

She *assumed* that she was not loved. She *assumed* that her lover was alive but did not want to see her. Her pain and suffering increased tremendously based on her assumptions.

She died in pain, felt worthless, felt sad, and felt totally abandoned.

Her energy and emotion did not go away after her death. It was passed in a vague form to her future self.

Perhaps, the future self (me) can heal the past.

Perhaps, the future self can learn lessons from the past, without needing to re-live the same scenario with different characters in this life.

Perhaps, there can be less pain and suffering now, and in the future.

Journey #5
05/04/08

It had been a hard week emotionally for me due to work. The messages I was getting in public and private were that:
"You are wasting time."
"This work is not good since there is no quick feedback."
"Give it up. Let the majority drive the direction."

I was angry and upset for while. *"How could they say such a thing?" "Can't they see the big picture?" "Why do they only look at short term items?" "Why do I have to deal with their negative energy?"*

I started doubting myself. Maybe they are right. I was upset that I was allowing their talk to impact my mood.

I asked myself, *"Why am I attracting these people now?"*
"What am I supposed to learn?"
"What message is for me?"

The following night, before going to bed, I asked for a dream to clarify the past week's experience. Early the next day, I had a dream that there was a party in my wife's parent's house. Several of my family was there. There was an acquaintance of mine whom I viewed as *flashy*, and a *show off*. He went to the basement of the house. The dinner was ready. I went down the basement with him. I told him dinner is ready. He said he *has to* pray before eating dinner. He told me to go upstairs. I knew he was not a religious person.

What did the dream convey to me? A person with a big ego *had to* do something to feel good in a public gathering.

Is that me that is taking this action or the other side in this reality? Am I being arrogant in hearing their criticism? Or is it due to their arrogance they are criticizing me? What old habits am I dealing with?

Next morning, in my meditation journey, I asked my guides to help me understand the dream better.

My guide asked me several questions, "*Is there something in your life that resembles their behavior at work? Are you looking at results in your spiritual journey with a short term point of view? Are you looking for a big event to validate your current efforts? Are you not looking at the big picture?*"

All of sudden a reality dawned on me. I was dealing with a similar situation on a different plane.

I told my guide, "Yes. I have been impatient with my spiritual progress this week."

I told my guide, "I was searching for a big affirmation to validate my efforts. I was judging my progress with a very short term perspective."

I told my guide, *"I was judging my co-workers lack of long term perspective while I was doing the same thing to myself."*

I told my guide, "Thank you!"

My guide said, "Be patient."
"Spirituality does not go on a linear path."
"Trust your instincts."
"Do not let the ego and old habits derail your progress."

Journey #6
05/16/08

I attended a group soul-retrieval and curse extraction ceremony.

We all lose a part of our soul due to trauma, and what we perceive to have happened to us. Soul-parts, depart from us to stay in safety. As a result, we feel emptiness inside. Soul-parts can return to us when we are ready to accept them.

A curse occurs due to past life events. A curse is a blocked energy that is burdening full development of a soul.

Shaman practitioners can do soul-retrieval and curse extraction.

The ceremony started.

A bit scared, and not knowing what to expect, I asked for help from my guides.

I felt knots in my lower abdomen. I also felt strong energy, around my throat before the start of the ceremony.

After going through smudging, clearing of energy fields, I was ready for the ceremony.

Blindfolded, I laid down, trusting the Universe for its grace and wisdom; I asked for the return of soul-parts that are best for my development at the time.

Drumming was powerful.

After a while, I felt the shaman by my side. She lightly touched my chest area. It felt like something was cutting me.

I felt something touch my hands and feet. As if someone was untying me.

After couple of seconds, I felt a strong heat and burning sensation around my heart.

Never have I felt this kind of sensation, and it lasted about 15 seconds.

Then, I felt either something entering my body, or leaving. I felt a great pressure on my rib cage. It felt like something pressing on it.

I did not know what was happening. I asked myself,
"Is this how dying feels?"
"What is the pressure?"

Scared and uncertain, I kept focusing on universal light for guidance and help. I kept hoping that I would not experience what I had just experienced again.

Finally the ceremony ended.

I felt like I was cut open and bleeding. The first thing I did, was touch my stomach area.

It was intact! But, I could still feel the pressure on my rib cage. The pressure subsided after many hours.

The shaman explained what she had seen during the curse extraction.

She told me that I had been a powerful man in an Egyptian tribe. My rival wanted to teach the tribal people a lesson. He tied my legs and feet. I was also tied tightly around the rib cage. I was made an example of what not to follow, by humiliating me. I eventually died due to wounds in my rib cage and dehydration.

She said, the energy for me from that life is *personal power*. By extraction of that curse I can more easily express in words or other forms my personal power.

She said, "Meditate on your experience. Ask questions. Get insights. It may take a while to feel the impact of the curse removal."

I have already felt the impact. I knew I was not the same person. I knew that emotions due to that experience, needed to be acknowledged and expressed over time.
I knew that I had survived the trauma, then and now. All I can do is, to own the emotions and grow from it.

I was excited by the prospect of having more energy and zest for expressing my personal power in this life time.

Although initially, I was shaken by the experience, I realized that sometimes one has to go through darkness to reach the light.

Journey #7
05/21/08

I asked to have a dream about my intent for the trance-journey the night before.

I had a dream about a *fountain pen*. Only that image remained with me when I woke up.

The intent of the trance-journey, was to journey on the message of the fountain pen.

After deep breathing and feeling the music for a while, I felt a jolt of energy in my heart and throat area.

I could feel the emotions inside me; joy and grief.

I could see the fountain pen writing. I could see the wet ink on a paper.

Seeing the ink, gave me the permission to express my feeling like the pen was doing through the ink.

I started laughing loudly, without concern for my surroundings.

I was watching the fountain pen writing. I was so amazed by the message in my dream.

I kept laughing from the depth of my being.

What a beautiful, and subtle way, to receive a message.

I kept laughing, deep, as if someone had pulled a funny trick on me.

After the while, laughter turned into loud crying.

Then, back to loud laughter.

The dance of laughter and crying, lasted a while until I became exhausted.

I expressed my emotions like a child without the burden of judgment.

I realized that there is a fine line between laughter and crying; it is sometimes hard to distinguish between them.

Journey #8
07/04/08

I was really upset by the death of my father-in-law.

I was preoccupied about my own eventual death with a lot of fear.

I decided to make a journey to the other side, to find ways to deal with my fear.

I asked permission from the guardian to enter the land of the departed.

It was cloudy and bit gloomy. The place was covered with gray crystals.

It reminded me of crystals that remove pain from the body.

As I walked further, the sky became lighter.

I reached the edge of a cliff. I saw a town in the valley below, with lots of lights.

I tried to get down there, but I could not. There was no path that I could see.

I finally asked my power animal (eagle), to take me down. He flew me down on his back.

There were several cement-type buildings. I felt that I could not enter them.

There were people with bright auras surrounding them. They were walking, but nobody noticed me or talked to me.

I asked the guardian, "How long will I be alive?"

He said, "For a while."

I asked, "How do I become less fearful of death?"

He said, "Live fully."

I thanked the guardian, returned to the physical world, and asked for confirmation within the next 24 hours about what I had heard.

In my meditations that day, and the next, I talked to my guides regarding my experiences. As soon I asked them mentally, my dog growled loudly both times. He has never done that, and did not repeat the growling again.

On the same day, while driving to the airport, there was talk on the radio of people thinking about death, and a lady asking people in the street, "If you are going to die, why do you want to live?"
Hearing that on the radio, gave me goose bumps.

The next day, I was in a book store waiting for my wife to finish her reading. I walked near a couple of books. One book attracted my attention. I read few pages. It was about how to live if you had a year left. The basic message was to live in the now.

The synchronicities that I encountered in 24 hours, totally confirmed to me my experience and the message was real.

Journey #9
08/08/08

The intent of this journey, was to meet my higher-self. I had a feeling of low spiritual energy, for the last past few days. It impacted my mood and my relationship with my wife.

Blindfolded, I listened to the music and started the journey.

I called upon my guides and spirits to help me on my journey, while doing regular deep breathing.

I was feeling sad, but I could not cry. I kept asking for help.

After a while, I started feeling tightness in my second and third chakras.

Feeling a bit frustrated, I decided to let go of my mind more, and focus totally on the music.

I got a sense of a very gentle, loving, and happy energy, in front of my mind's eye.

It was a wonderful, joyful, energy that made me feel an unconditional love.

I realized how low my spiritual-energy was, compared to the loving energy.

I cried loudly like a little child.

I felt blessed and loved.

I also felt ashamed of thinking that I was not lovable for the past couple of days.

I danced with the beautiful energy while crying and sometimes laughing.

Later, I also danced with my guides. They all had smiles on their faces.

I then sensed a different energy in my mind's eye. This was similar to the energy that I sense when I ask the Universe to transform my negative energy into a positive one.

While putting my face on the ground, sobbing, I asked the Universe to recycle my negative energy that was in my body.

After a while, exhausted, I laid down on the floor.

I was peaceful, despite the sharp pain I felt in my stomach.

I was sweating. I could feel the love and joy around me. I felt a tingly sensation around my heart.

I was reminded that I had a *choice* to stay at a lower energy level, or could tap into the Universal energy, that I currently felt.

After the journey, I felt like a new person.

Journey #10
08/14/08

I started my journey, by asking for protection from the Universe.

The intent of this journey, was to ask forgiveness from my sister for saying things to her as a child that hurt her, and continues to have an impact on her now.

Lying on my back, I started the journey.

I received a clear message that I have to forgive first, before asking for forgiveness.

Asking for forgiveness is easy. I have to forgive first to show the Universe that I am sincere.

All of sudden, I realized forgiving is not easy.

It felt like forgiving was like spending money when you feel you do not have enough of it.

What power did *not forgiving* give me that I resisted forgiving?

I had a big *"aha."*

If I forgive, then I lose the power to be a victim. I had NOBODY else to blame!

I went through the process of forgiving my sister for hurt she may have inflicted on me as a child. I then asked for her forgiveness.

We then embraced each other, emotions overcome me.

I went through the same process with my father, whom I always thought I had forgiven.

I realized that my verbal forgiveness, sometimes was not sincere. I had resisted forgiving completely, people that I thought I had forgiven already!

I also realized that forgiving is a process that needs to be repeated. We may forgive at one level, but need to repeat it at deeper levels. As we forgive more, we receive a deeper healing.

Self-Healing Techniques

The techniques on the following pages presume the reader to have basic meditation experience. Please utilize any basic meditation techniques to provide yourself a foundation. Several meditation techniques, as used by the author, are described.

Changing Your Belief
11/22/07

You realize that you have a belief that no longer serves you.

The belief needs to be changed at the subconscious level.

Go in a meditative state; ask your guide to help you.

A guide can be a man or woman, but needs to have feminine attributes (language of subconscious).

Subconscious is typically represented by a tunnel, stairs, or rock.

Enter your subconscious by entering a tunnel inside the ground; there are many rooms in the tunnel; ask your guide to lead you to the *room of beliefs*.

After walking through many tunnels, she will stop by that room; go inside that room, you will see many books on various beliefs.

If you want to change your belief on *destiny*, find the book on *destiny* in that room, find the page that has the specific belief that you want to change.

Read the page first, put a big X on that page; tear it out and burn it.

Write down your new belief in the book; make sure it's wording is close to the previous wording; for example: changing from, *I can not choose my destiny* to, *I can choose my destiny*.

Walk out with your guide, from the tunnel and thank your guide.

After meditation, make sure you write down your new belief on paper, and place it where you can see and read it often.

You need to remind your subconscious that you are serious about your new belief, by often repeating the new belief.

Forgiveness Meditation
03/01/08

This is a trip to the valley of forgiveness.

Begin your meditation. Start from a safe place in your mind.

Ask your guides for help in your journey.

Go beyond the bond of safety in your meditation.

Imagine yourself walking in the countryside. You are in unfamiliar territory.

Continue your path, over a great hill, and see down beneath, there is a beautiful valley.

You are now in the valley. There are many colorful flowers.

You will pick a bouquet of flowers.

The first area you see has a vast amount of red flowers. Pick 3 or 4 red flowers.

The next area you see has a vast amount of orange flowers. Pick 3 or 4 orange flowers.

The next area you see has a vast amount of yellow flowers. Pick 3 or 4 yellow flowers.

The next area you see has a vast amount of green ferns. Pick 3 or 4 green ferns.

The next area you see has a vast amount of blue flowers. Pick 3 or 4 blue flowers.

The next area you see has a vast amount of Indigo flowers. Pick 3 or 4 indigo flowers.

The next area you see has a vast amount of violet flowers. Pick 3 or 4 violet flowers.

Look up and see a disk (wood, metal, or granite) on the side of a hill.

Walk up toward the hill; imagine the other person (or yourself) on the other side of the disk.

The other person may be ugly looking, and in torment.

Place the flowers down on the disk; visualize that they transform into a translucent colored sphere.

Pick the sphere up; toss it upward to the other person.

The sphere will cover the person up; you see him changing through the translucence.

Take one step forward and say, "*I forgive you.*"

Take another step and say, "*I forgive you.*"
You will see changes in him.

Repeat walking toward him several more steps and say again, "*I forgive you.*"

You will see that the other person is gradually changing. He is no longer ugly and hurting.

If the person is you, then put your arms around yourself, and bring yourself inside your being, inside your self

If the person in front of you is someone you care about, then hug him.

If the person in front of you is someone you do not want to have any more dealings with, then turn your back and go in the other direction.

Processing Feelings
05/17/07

Processing feelings are a very important aspect of our daily interactions.

It is extremely important to be able to constructively respond to our feelings.

There are fours steps involved.

Step 1: Recognize the feeling. Are you sad, happy, or angry?

Step 2: Feel the feeling deeply within you, without any judgment.

Step 3: Cleanly express the feeling. This is in a meditative state most of the time.

Step 4: Release the feeling; turn your attention away, and do not focus on that issue any more.

For example, you are driving on a road and a driver cuts in front of you.

  Step 1: Recognize that you feel angry or scared.

  Step 2: Feel the fear and anger inside you. Experience it for a short time, telling yourself, *"It is okay to be angry."*

Step 3: Visualize the person in front of you. Tell him, "You are a good person. Your behavior is reckless and scares me. Your behavior can create bodily harm to yourself and others. I feel anger for your behavior."

Step 4: Release the feeling of anger and fear, and focus on something else. If this process is done effectively, you should have no lingering emotional anger based on the incident.

Depending on depth of your emotions, you may need to repeat the above steps several times, in order to completely acknowledge and dissolve those feelings.

What Has Made You a Prisoner?
09/17/08

This exercise is for discovering what has stunted your spiritual growth.

Relax. Get ready to mediate.

In a meditative state, ask your guide for help, to accompany you to meet the keeper of your subconscious.

Go down a tunnel with your guide.

You will encounter the keeper of your subconscious. Tell her that something in there has made you a prisoner.

Ask the keeper to guide you to a place where part of you is being kept as a prisoner.

Follow the keeper closely; she may walk swiftly. She may take you to a jail.

Ask for the key to unlock the jail cell.

Ask the keeper to guide the part of you that is in the jail cell, to safety.

Go back with the keeper and the guide, to the tunnel where you started your journey. Thank your guide, and the keeper for their help.

Try to get a sense of what has imprisoned part of you. Look for signs when you are awake or dreaming.

The signs may point you to your attitude, belief, etc.

Cube of Success
11/07/07

This exercise is to obtain an understanding of your current success in life, and perhaps how you can enhance your success more.

Go into a meditative state.

Walk to your safe place. Drift beyond the safety.

You do not know where you are going.

You come down to a house. It looks like a cube.

This is your *cube of success.*

Ask your higher-self to help you with this exercise.

How big is the cube?
Where is it located?
How is the foundation?
Is it on a flat surface, or on a hill?

Enter the cube with your higher-self.

Feel the energy of the cube.

Is it easy to get in or out?
Is the roof high or low?

Sit down with your higher-self and the symbol of your success (perhaps another person), and talk about the success cube.

Ask their opinion.

They may ask you to move the cube to a different place.

They may ask you to make the base of the cube stronger.

You may also do things to the cube based on your intuition.

Drift back to your safe place.

Visit your cube of success as needed.

Index

Abandon, 85, 91, 96, 130

Adolescent, 69, 75, 97, 98, 99, 206

Angry, 32, 53, 63, 64, 77, 78, 83, 86, 103, 128, 129, 137, 171, 176, 188, 195, 206, 237, 280, 281

April writings, 43, 71, 142, 204, 206, 228

Assumption, 31, 73, 74, 113, 219, 226, 254

Attachments, 32, 196, 197

August writings, 70, 132, 149, 173, 174, 215, 230, 233, 268, 271

Belief, 17, 19, 22, 23, 31, 32, 33, 34, 35, 37, 39, 40, 41, 43, 44, 45, 46, 47, 51, 52, 53, 54, 55, 56, 57, 58, 59, 60, 61, 62, 63, 64, 65, 66, 67, 68, 69, 70, 71, 72, 73, 74, 75, 76, 77, 78, 79, 80, 81, 82, 83, 84, 88, 92, 101, 103, 104, 105, 113, 116, 117, 119, 125, 128, 129, 132, 133, 135, 140, 165, 166, 172, 175, 176, 177, 181, 182, 187, 190, 192, 199, 200, 205, 212, 213, 219, 220, 226, 234, 236, 237, 238, 254, 273, 275, 276, 278, 281, 283

Blame, 34, 74, 86, 136, 173, 174, 176, 182, 206, 271

Communities within communities, 206

Companion, 77, 78, 111

Control, 34, 44, 110, 113, 115, 165, 175, 176, 188, 200, 206

Death, 29, 31, 46, 101, 120, 132, 136, 195, 210, 219, 243, 244, 248, 254, 265, 266

December writings, 79, 122, 123, 125, 194, 195, 198, 226

Destiny, 29, 32, 252, 275, 276

Dream interpretation, 163

Dream role play, 167

Dreams, 158, 159, 160, 163, 165, 167

Drum beats, 151

Eagle, 153, 154, 155, 156, 157, 220, 265

Ego, 30, 41, 45, 46, 47, 50, 51, 53, 62, 77, 113, 132, 190, 195, 210, 226, 247, 257, 258

Embrace, 113, 116, 131, 219, 220

Emotions, 16, 17, 18, 19, 22, 23, 31, 33, 35, 37, 39, 45, 46, 47, 50, 51, 53, 54, 58, 59, 60, 63, 64, 70, 77, 78, 81, 87, 89, 90, 92, 94, 98, 99, 103, 109, 111, 113, 115, 116, 117, 119, 120, 122, 123, 124, 125, 128, 129,

130, 134, 137, 138, 142,
159, 163, 171, 175, 176,
177, 178, 179, 188, 195,
199, 202, 203, 206, 207,
211, 213, 218, 222, 226,
232, 240, 241, 243, 247,
249, 250, 251, 252, 254,
261, 262, 263, 264, 265,
268, 269, 272, 273, 280, 281
Empower, 115
Expectations, 44, 116, 117,
143, 150, 178, 202, 206
Express, 17, 50, 86, 103, 113,
120, 129, 156, 165, 171,
177, 204, 206, 216, 232,
240, 261, 263, 280
Fate, 29, 137
Father, 17, 18, 43, 101, 105,
106, 176, 208, 265, 272
Fear, 19, 31, 35, 45, 46, 47, 50,
51, 63, 77, 78, 103, 109,
110, 111, 112, 113, 114,
115, 116, 117, 124, 159,
171, 188, 199, 207, 218,
247, 249, 265, 280, 281
February writings, 105, 161,
163, 165, 167, 182, 202,
213, 222, 249
Forgiving, 119, 138, 180, 181,
271, 272, 273, 278, 279
God, 17, 19, 22, 23, 34, 37, 39,
40, 41, 47, 53, 54, 55, 56,
57, 58, 60, 70, 71, 72, 75,
76, 77, 78, 79, 80, 81, 82,
83, 84, 88, 103, 104, 111,
119, 128, 143, 175, 177, 234

Gratitude, 134, 190, 232, 239,
240, 241, 242, 250
Grief, 127, 130, 132, 134
Grieving, 107, 136
Grieving process, 127
Grow, 24, 37, 87, 107, 114,
134, 178, 207, 262
Hell, 55, 62, 63, 182, 220
Helpless, 39, 136, 192
Identity, 39, 81
Inner child, 16, 30, 43, 70, 85,
86, 87, 89, 91, 92, 94, 96,
97, 98, 111, 127, 130, 135,
137, 138, 143, 192, 196,
201, 236
Insights, 184, 185, 186, 188,
190, 192, 194, 195, 196,
198, 200, 204, 206, 208,
210, 212, 213, 215, 239, 240
Ironic, 185
January writings, 113, 130,
140, 159, 196, 246, 248
Journey, 15, 16, 17, 19, 66,
118, 119, 149, 150, 177,
194, 197, 246, 248, 249,
251, 256, 257, 259, 263,
265, 268, 270, 271, 277, 283
Judgment, 45, 67, 70, 128,
131, 144, 171, 196, 207,
219, 220, 228
July writings, 22, 37, 119,
171, 217, 239, 265
June Writings, 24, 39, 58, 64,
134, 172, 184, 212, 236,
241, 243
Letting go, 195

Life, 22, 24, 25, 26, 27, 29, 30,
31, 32, 33, 34, 50, 77, 137,
214, 220, 251, 252, 257,
258, 275, 276
Love, 16, 17, 18, 31, 37, 39, 45,
46, 48, 53, 54, 58, 59, 60,
70, 87, 89, 90, 94, 98, 99,
109, 111, 112, 113, 118,
119, 120, 121, 122, 123,
124, 125, 130, 134, 137,
138, 142, 175, 176, 177,
178, 195, 202, 203, 211,
222, 243, 247, 250, 252,
254, 268, 269
March writings, 48, 73, 188,
200, 208, 210, 277
Martyr, 23, 140, 141, 142
May writings, 29, 56, 60, 86,
151, 153, 185, 211, 256,
259, 263, 280
Meditation, 72, 89, 94, 97,
150, 162, 166, 194, 246,
248, 249, 251, 256, 259,
263, 265, 268, 271, 278, 282
Mother, 18, 43, 98, 107, 134,
135, 136, 137, 151, 176,
201, 208
Navigations within, 147, 148,
149, 153, 158, 159, 160,
161, 163, 164, 165
New Year wish, 198
November writings, 50, 68,
192, 275, 284
October writings, 35, 53, 62,
66, 77, 101, 103, 178, 190

Other influencers, 17, 22, 23,
44, 54, 55, 56, 57, 71, 101,
103, 104, 105, 113, 185
Pain, 67, 70, 103, 105, 106,
200, 201, 228, 245, 251,
253, 254, 255, 265, 269
Perspective, 29, 30, 31, 32, 50,
77, 220, 251, 257, 258
Prison Guard, 208
Purpose, 17, 19, 22, 30, 31, 54,
64, 66, 67, 69, 88, 211
Recognize, 17, 129, 171, 207,
216, 280
Re-Entering dreams, 165
Relationships, 75, 116, 122,
134, 171, 172, 173, 174,
178, 180, 182, 213, 268, 277
Release, 84
Remind me, 76, 81, 82, 83
Responsibility, 45, 67, 83,
157, 173, 174, 178, 213, 215
Savior, 23, 140, 141, 206
Self-Healing techniques, 89,
91, 94, 97, 99, 127, 275,
277, 280, 282, 284, 285
Self-Pity, 22, 39, 70, 136, 139,
140, 141, 142, 144, 173,
201, 206, 271
September writings, 81, 89,
92, 94, 97, 116, 120, 127,
186, 219, 224, 282
Shamanism, 147, 148, 149,
151, 153
Shame, 86, 92, 94, 95, 176
Should, 43, 64, 70, 71, 79, 101,
128, 133, 135, 181, 200,
236, 237, 238, 281

Suffering, 200, 201, 228, 245, 254, 255
Teacher, 17, 22, 23, 44, 54, 55, 56, 57, 71, 103, 104, 105, 113, 185
Totem animals, 153, 154, 155, 156, 157, 220, 249, 265
Trance, 15, 149, 263
Victim, 23, 39, 70, 136, 140, 141, 142, 144, 173, 201, 206, 271
Who am I?, 43, 45, 48, 50

Resources that helped the author are locate at:
www.shervinhojat.com

Notes:

www.ingramcontent.com/pod-product-compliance
Lightning Source LLC
Chambersburg PA
CBHW071651090426
42738CB00009B/1493